Praise For Ro

Buster has been a wonderful partner and my best friend. He always wanted the best for our children and me, so he worked hard to provide a good living for us. I am proud to be married to him for 60 years.
—Hazel (Roberts) Strickland

Because my father does not meet strangers, he met friends easily and quickly in Phoenix and accepted his new path in life head on.
—Marilyn Jean Livingston

My father is a very compassionate man. Besides being there consistently for his family, he visits the sick and shut in on a regular basis…always helping others.
—Rochelle Aloise (Strickland) Hawthorne

At an early age my Dad taught me that hard work was necessary to become successful in life. My Dad is a workaholic and a provider; but he is also gentle, caring and fun loving.
—Kenneth Leon Strickland

I really admired Buster for being able to overcome his medical condition. He could have given up so easily, but he didn't. Instead he demonstrated courage and strength, and went on to lead a very productive life.
—Arthur E. Strickland

Whenever I see Buster, I know it's going to be a wonderful experience; he always makes you feel like royalty.
—Helen Strickland

Uncle Buster is one of the nicest, most hard-working, busiest human beings you'll ever meet. He, truly, is his brother's keeper.
—Yvonne Strickland David

Thank you for being such an inspiration to the Roberts Family since marrying my sister. Thanks for being the husband that you are, the father that you are and the special brother-in-law that you have been to me. Thank you Buster for keeping our family close, even though we are many miles apart.
—Frances (Roberts) Brim

Hazel and Buster have been a blessing to each other, during their sixty years of marriage, as they have been a blessing to others during their lives.
—Gentry (and Elaine) Roberts

I commend Buster for his dedication, perseverance and the difference he has made in so many lives by caring, and sharing with a willing heart and a big smile.
—Pearl (Roberts) Abercrombie

He is woven into the Roberts family as if he was born to be in it. If I had to give him a recommendation, I would say "Robuster is the best brother anyone could ever have!" He's super!
—Aaron Roberts

No one is ever a stranger to Buster and he will do anything he can for you. He is a kind, giving and unselfish person. I think that is the secret to his blessings and success in life.
—Mabel (Roberts) Richardson

I always go by my own instincts; when you see a nice person you just want to say "Hello". I remember telling someone from Barry Goldwater's company that I wanted to meet that young man over there. Buster and I were introduced and have been friends ever since.
—Virginia M. Ullman

Buster is a wonderful friend and has helped and supported us always. He makes taking care of us important and always finds a solution to a problem.
—Mr. & Mrs. Pritzlaff

It's been ten years that I've know Buster; I still run into him at an occasional party and he has not changed; he always greets me with a big smile and makes me feel like I'm part of his extended family.
   —Claire Newton

With or without a title, you were special and had to be a part of his very large family, which includes a lot of people across "the valley" (Phoenix).
   —Trisha Ann Garrett

Buster is my family and he has touched me in many ways with his knowledge and wisdom. I admire him because he is a truly blessed man.
   —Priscilla Krucko

In my twelve plus years of knowing him, Buster has always had some good advice. He uses his experience to help guide those of us who ask, in order to keep us out of the pitfalls.
   —Nazim Muhammad

Nothing is too big or too little for Buster. He stands tall with the greats and puts his hands out to the oppressed. He never helps people for praise, but just because they need him.
   —Cathy Bua

Buster knows everyone in the room, and when he speaks to you, you are the only one that matters.
   —Bennie Bua

If Buster called upon me at two o'clock in the morning, I'd be there in a heartbeat.
   —Chuck Hahn

Uncle Buster loves a challenge and doesn't hesitate to try out something new.
   —Annette Willis

I have always found "Buster" to be a true reliable friend who can be called upon whether the need is personal, that of the organization, or from the community at large.
—Ananias Mason

From the moment I met "Bus" (all his close friends call him that) I knew he was going to be a friend for life.
—Mike Gordon

Buster has touched my life in many ways, but the most wonderful way was when he played the role of cupid. I had no dreams that this man would structure my life as he did.
—Bettye Mallette

I think of Mr. Strickland and his lovely wife, Mrs. Hazel Strickland as my adopted parents. I am grateful that God has blessed me to know them…they took me back to the "old school" when families showed "love for people in their community."
—Fannie Jackson

What a blessing it is to know Buster Strickland and I thank God for the influence he has had in my life.
—William C. "Bill" Smith III

Buster has always been nothing but kind to this family and we love him to no end.
—Judy Sutter (Judy) and Family

Buster is always the first one to help someone in trouble; no one has a bigger heart.
—Margie McHarg

LED BY THE SPIRIT

A Sharecropper's Son Tells His Story of Love,
Happiness, Survival and Success

By Robuster Strickland
With Yvonne Rose

Strickland Books

Phoenix

LED BY THE SPIRIT: A Sharecropper's Son Tells His Story of Love, Happiness, Survival and Success

By Robuster Strickland
with Yvonne Rose

Published by:
Strickland Books
Phoenix, AZ 85048

Buster Strickland, Publisher   Virginia M. Ullman, Associate Publisher
Yvonne Rose, Editor   The Printed Page, Interior & Cover Design

Dedication

I dedicate this book to my late grandson Jason "Robuster" Livingston, who was named after me. Sadly, he got his wings on my birthday, November 4, 2001. We will continue to celebrate Jason's life, along with my birth.

Acknowledgments

Words cannot express my sincere thanks to my lovely wife Hazel, who has been my inspiration throughout our sixty years of marriage.

My children, grandchildren and great grandchildren have always been supportive and loving throughout those seasons of my life. I'd like to leave this thought with them "If you want to reap the harvest, you have to plant a seed. And if I can help someone along life's journey then my living will not have been in vain."

I'd like to thank my pastor, Dr. Warren H. Stewart, Sr. who has been supportive of my writing this book. Truly, he has been a blessing to my family and me. We love you Pastor Stewart. Many blessings on you and your family.

To my family and the many friends who we have met in Arizona over the past 55 years. Thank you for your love, loyalty, friendship and support.

To Virginia Ullman, a special thanks to you for sharing the vision. We'll always remember you.

And I would like to give praise to Yvonne Rose, Vice President and Senior Editor of Amber Books. Without her expertise, talent and writing skills, this book would not have been written. Thank you, Yvonne. It has been a pleasure. I'll always be grateful to you.

I will forever be grateful for God's love and for the strength and guidance that He gives me each day, enabling me to live my life to the fullest.

—Robuster "Buster" Strickland

My heartfelt thanks to Buster and his beautiful wife Hazel for making me a part of their family and entrusting me to communicate their story; and to my wonderful husband Tony for sharing his wisdom with me, encouraging me to accept every challenge as a new opportunity and helping me realize that every word I write can make a difference in someone's life.

—Yvonne Rose

Contents

Foreword

Like virtually all of the names of prominent persons in the Bible have symbolic significance, so does the given name of *a sharecropper's son who tells his story of survival and success* in this book. From his mother's womb to this very day, Robuster "Buster" Strickland has lived a life characterized by strength, endurance, fullness and vitality in spite of formidable challenges to his health, heart and heritage as an African American born in the South during Jim Crow days in America. This real-life saga of the seventh son born to James and Sarah Strickland is inspiring, intriguing and, at times, inexplicable as it relates to the many, marked paths Robuster's life has taken him all headed in a forward direction.

Serving as the senior pastor of Brother Strickland and his wonderful wife of more than sixty years, Sister Hazel Roberts Strickland, all of the nearly 30 years I have pastored the First Institutional Baptist Church of Phoenix, Arizona, has enabled me to know, admire and appreciate them and their family. The love story of Robuster and Hazel needs to be read and told over and over again to give hope and direction to current and future generations who have been reared in our "divorce court culture" that hardly blinks an eye at the long-term damage that marital break-ups inflict upon families, communities and our society as a whole. Moreover, Buster's love for the Lord and his church has made him an almost permanent fixture in the pews at First Institutional since he united as a member in 1949. It has been my privilege to share many meaningful life experiences with the Stricklands, which have brought joy on most occasions and sorrow during a few trying times this side of the Jordan River.

As a disciple of Jesus Christ I do *not* believe in luck. *Providence*—the faith that God is providing for His children every step of the way—is my Biblical and theological alternative to chance. The contents of this autobiography of a seasoned Christian man who has been a loving and providing husband, father, grandfather, friend, confidante, employee and church member give incident after incident when nothing but God's hand has guided Robuster Strickland by *divine providence.*

My prayer is that not only will Buster be *led by the Spirit,* but every man, woman, boy and girl who reads this book, so that they will know beyond a shadow of a doubt that our Creator-God does *lead by His Spirit* all who will follow him.

> Dr. Warren H. Stewart, Sr.
> Senior Pastor
> First Institutional Baptist Church
> Phoenix, Arizona

Introduction - Led By the Spirit

My life has always been far from ordinary; I grew up the son of a sharecropper, and as one of my dad's twenty children. My parents taught us good values, discipline and responsibility; they helped me to be humble and constantly demonstrated the goodness of sharing.

Five years after I married the most wonderful woman in the world, I was told by my doctor that I had only one year to live. With a young wife and a beautiful baby girl to care for, I had to make a major decision that would change our lives forever.

I have accepted many challenges and overcome many obstacles. But, I have always been a firm believer in God and felt that He would see me through if I followed His teachings.

I feel so blessed and thankful that I was allowed to live my life to the fullest and have continued to ask God to guide me in His work and with His word.

—Robuster Strickland

Part One

To believe is to know that every day is a new beginning.
It is to trust that miracles happen, and dreams really do come true.
To believe is to know the value of a nurturing heart,
The innocence of a child's eyes and the beauty of an aging hand,
For it is through their teachings we learn to love.
To believe is to find the strength and courage that lies within us.
When it is time to pick up the pieces and begin again.
To believe is to know we are not alone,
That life is a gift and this is our time to cherish it.
To believe is to know that wonderful surprises are just waiting to happen,
And all our hopes and dreams are within reach.
If only we believe.

—Author Unknown

Chapter 1
Divine Providence

I may never know why I went out that night;
but I like to think it was "Divine Providence".

June 6, 1998 was a typical hot Arizona summer night—the temperature had been in the 100's all day. Around 10:00PM, I was watching television, became very restless, couldn't relax, and couldn't get cool.

I had endured the Arizona temperatures for almost fifty years, but for some reason, on this particular night, the heat was almost unbearable. I really needed to cool off, so I decided to go where I knew the air conditioning would be on full blast.

You see, I lived about five or six miles from the Gila River Casino in Arizona and every once in a while, I go out to play the "Wheel of Fortune"—but never this late at night. I thought this would be a nice break for about an hour or so, never dreaming it would turn out to be an all night ordeal.

I had asked my wife Hazel to go with me; but she said she preferred to stay home. So, I went out alone armed with a one hundred-dollar bill and twelve singles—I figured that would be enough to lose in one night.

When I arrived at the casino, I encountered a little old lady who was sitting at the one-dollar progressive slot machines, crying over the fact that she had just lost $200 of her $250 welfare check. I felt bad, but since she was no longer gambling, asked her if I could use the machine. She reluctantly moved, complaining all the while.

I changed my singles first, into twelve one-dollar tokens, and then proceeded to fill the slots with the first three. On the first pull, I won $400 and the little old lady who had stayed to watch started yelling, "That' my money! He's got my money!" The security guards came; and after I explained the scenario they promptly disembarked, only to return a few moments later.

I slipped another three coins into the slots, the machine froze and the bells and whistles went off. When the security guards arrived for the second time, I jubilantly told them that I had just won $100,000; and they recanted by telling me, "No, you didn't!" As I became more and more confused, I heard someone in the background say, "You just won a million dollars!"

I was in shock and couldn't respond, but I called my wife Hazel. She thought I was pulling a prank; so I called my son Kenneth who then called his mother and they both came right over to the casino. In the meantime, I managed to dial some other family members—my niece Yvonne, my sister-in-law Helen and my granddaughter Tamra and her husband Paul—who all arrived promptly. (I was delighted to give the little old lady back her lost money, plus a bonus).

In no time at all, the security guards had roped off the area where my slot machine was and called in the technical specialist from Reno, Nevada. They asked me if I wanted to come back in the morning because it would be a long ordeal. Quite naturally, time didn't matter and four and a half hours later, I signed the winning documents, received a check and left the casino as a new millionaire.

As a husband and father, I had worked hard to take care of Hazel and the children; they were my responsibility and I always wanted the best for them. It has always felt good to be able to help other family members and friends, too, whenever possible; as well as those community people and charitable organizations that needed a helping hand or some food on their table.

This wonderful gift offered me an opportunity beyond my wildest dreams. I gave my family members a tidy sum, donated some of the proceeds to my church's building fund and contributed money to a number of charitable organizations.

I have always prayed for a way to help those in need and God has always answered my prayers. This is my story ......

Chapter 2
Robuster Strickland

My legal name is Robuster Strickland, but everyone calls me "Buster". I was born in Patrick County, Virginia in 1923 and weighed 11 pounds and 13 ounces at birth—and that was without a Cesarean. When he delivered me, the doctor made a comment to my mother: "My, he is a robust baby, isn't he?" So that's how I was named Robuster.

I am the son of James Monroe Strickland and Sarah Smith Strickland. James Strickland was African American and Cherokee Indian. Sarah Smith Strickland was African American and German American. I would be the last child born to my mother and father Sarah and James Strickland while they lived in the South.

A sharecropper in North Carolina, my Dad, James Strickland had twenty children. Seven children—three boys and four girls—were borne by his first wife (Gertrude Penn). After Gertrude died of complications from pneumonia, Dad met my mother and, shortly thereafter, they were married. Dad had thirteen more children with my mother, his second wife, Sarah. I was Dad's 7th son and the 7th child borne to Sarah and James Strickland.

Chapter 3
Sarah and James Strickland

James Monroe Strickland was born December 5, 1867. Sarah Jane Smith was born December 22, 1891. Sarah was only eighteen years old when she met James, but was very smitten with him; she lovingly accepted all his children. A year later, the couple started a family of their own. Sarah gave birth to thirteen children, which would have brought the total headcount to twenty. Sadly, though, five of them died, either at birth or when they were infants.

My parents were among the hundreds of African American men and women who led the way as sharecroppers in North Carolina and Virginia. What happened to them happened to most of the black sharecroppers or "land owners" in America. Their land was lost because of a lack of communication between the banker and the land-owner. The depression was approaching; living was rough and money was tight; the farmers were given little or no notice to pay off their indebtedness to the bank or lose their property. As fate would have it; James and Sarah Strickland would lose their land because they were a day late making the mortgage payment.

The first black farmers, many who were descendants of slaves, began moving to the Chestnut Ridge (Mount Airy) area of North Carolina in the late 1800's. They were allotted a parcel of land to work the fields owned by the white farmers (planters) and the "rent" would come out of the sharecroppers (black farmers) made from selling the crops.

The camaraderie that existed between families allowed them to manage and survive on these farms. They shared the responsibility of building one-room log cabins and clearing the land for farming.

Saws and axes were the main tools used to raise a cabin; it took about a week to build. Red mud was used to seal up the cracks; shingles rived from chestnut trees by hand were used for roofing.

As one family would prepare to build cabins, barns, pack-houses and sheds, the community would come together for a "chopping" to clear the land and prepare the wood.

Once land was cleared, crops of tobacco, corn, sweet potato and other foods and staples were planted. They had no machinery for farming, their sole way of surviving.

At first, many families slept on the floor and kept warm by a small fireplace. If they had a light, it came from a small lantern. Much of the material for clothing was made from sacks; and the clothes were handed down until they fell apart. They were then cut into squares that the women would sew together to make quilts during the winter quilting. The women would also prepare the food while the men worked together planning, establishing goals and creating visions for the future. Churches and schoolhouses were some of the results of their plans.

James and his family had moved several times while trying to make ends meet by sharecropping in the various tobacco fields in Mount Airy, North Carolina along the Virginia State border in Patrick County. James found it pretty rough to raise a big family, while working as a sharecropper in the South during the early 1900's; and he consistently ran into racial problems. Typically, plantation owners exploited the system to their advantage, and most sharecroppers or tenants often ended up in debt at the end of each year. This scenario was repeated year after year for James Strickland and his family.

With no income during the off-season, tenants like the Stricklands were forced to buy food, clothing and other necessary supplies on credit from the plantation commissaries. Prices were excessive, goods were inferior and debt piled up. When harvest time came around, tenants were often forced to sell their share of the crop directly to the plantation at below market prices. After the harvest, the tenants often failed to earn enough to cover their debts.

James Monroe Strickland had worked in those tobacco fields for nine years, managing to make enough payments to finally purchase the one hundred acres of land that he and his family lived on—that was rightfully earned from sharecropping over the years. Without notification, James was told that he had one payment left on the property, which needed to be paid by midnight of that same day. But before 6 o'clock in the evening, the owner came, unannounced, to collect the mortgage payment; and James didn't have the full final payment for the property. The landlord was so cruel, that he ripped up the deed right there on the spot.

James Monroe Strickland's life flashed before him—his years of blood, sweat and tears—the disappointment that he knew he would see in the eyes of his wife and children. He was very angry with the landlord, but there was not too much he could do about it. In the 1920s, the threat of racial violence loomed over the South and Negroes tried not to challenge white people because they lived in fear of mob violence, lynching and the Ku Klux Klan. But, James could not and would not control his anger—he was so angry that he began an argument or some type of altercation, which resulted in a fight with the landlord.

James Strickland won the battle, but needless to say, lost the land. In a way, he had already made up his mind that he would have to make arrangements to relocate his family. So, when the time came, he was prepared. After the altercation, he knew he had to leave North Carolina immediately, because he would never get a fair trial in the South. So, without delay, James Monroe Strickland gathered his family and left, to move up North.

James would never look back.... and was determined to find peace, prosperity and comfort for himself and his family in Long Island, New York.

Chapter 4

New York...At Last

It was 1926 and I was two years old when we got to Long Island. For years, my dad managed to carve us out a meager existence when he worked on potato farms in Laurel and Mattituck. With help from my mother and all the older children (most could work) it was a little easier to survive on the farms. But, in Long Island, we could only work the farm during the Spring, Summer and Fall. When it got cold in the wintertime, there wasn't too much else to do, so most of the family worked on duck farms. We also did odd jobs for different people, such as cleaning their yards, housework, shoveling snow and property maintenance.

All together my mother and father had twenty children -10 boys and 10 girls between them. We were barely two years apart. Most of us to be healthy adults; but unfortunately, during my childhood, three of my brothers and sisters died tragically from pneumonia and other respiratory ailments. At the age of two, I had also developed an asthma condition, so my work status would be limited and my life would be constantly challenged.

While I was growing up, my family lived a mile from the schoolhouse. Fortunately, we all went to the same school. By the age of six, when I started school I had developed asthma so bad that I could not walk far. My brothers and sisters had to take turns pulling me in my little red wagon to school. I didn't go out to recess to play like the other children I stayed in school or in the cafeteria for recess. After school, it was the same routine with the wagon; this continued for about four years. By the time, I was in the 5th grade, somehow, my health began to improve; for no unknown reason my asthma was just easing up and I was beginning to get better.

There were at least seven of us in school at any given time, so even with help from the older children, it wasn't easy for mother and father to feed, clothe and keep clean clothes on everyone. My mother would make quilts and clothes for all of us in her spare time.

After school, we'd all have chores to do. Our chores were equally distributed between the family members. My chores were simple like: washing the dishes, bringing in some wood, sweeping the floors, cleaning the house, helping to cook (which I especially enjoyed) and things like that. My mother, of course, would do the majority of the cooking with the help of my sisters. Cooking and preparing food for the entire family was a major chore—most of the time there were at least seven kids, plus my mother and father at all times. You can imagine how much preparation it took to feed a whole family that size, and it never failed. My mother prepared three meals a day, seven days a week.

When it came down to eating, it really helped to live on a farm; most of our food was raised there. We grew all types of vegetables and we'd have our own milk, eggs and butter. Most of the meats we ate came from the cows, chickens and pigs right there on the farm. We did not own the farm, but we worked for the owner and got paid weekly.

Potatoes were a chief crop on Long Island; potato picking was really fun. On a good day, our family would range an average of picking one acre of potatoes a day. We would pick the potatoes and put them into large burlap bags. After we picked our quota of potatoes for the farmer, there were always a few left on the field; so the farmer would let our family go into the fields and pick potatoes for ourselves. We picked and saved so many bags for the winter—we all had plenty to eat. We, usually, had at least 200 large burlap bags of potatoes left through and after the winter, so my dad turned it into a small business. Ironically, he would sell the same potatoes back to the boss after we cut them and made them ready to be planted in the spring.

The potatoes had to be cut into sections with at least an eye or two on every section before being planted in the ground in the spring. We would then cut the potatoes out in the sections and sell them back to the farmer to be planted—it would help the farmer and help us financially. This was not the only vegetable left in the fields; there was also cabbage, broccoli, brussel sprouts , peas and so forth. Before the farmers plowed them under, the farmer would tell us to help ourselves. We were always available to help ourselves and that's how we managed to get and stay ahead. My mother would use strawberries and all types of fruit to make jams and preservatives in jars and cans—so you see we always had plenty of food to eat.

On Long Island sound in the Peconic Bay/Atlantic Ocean fishing was very, very good on the boats as well as on the shores. It was wonderful on the island and fish was plentiful; we dug up clams, oysters, mussels, scallops, crabs, eels, and all kinds of fish.

Chapter 5
Small Towns and Big Winds

Most of my older brothers and sisters, born to Gertrude (James' first wife) and James Strickland, grew up in Virginia. Their names were: Roscoe, Cora, Donie, Dorthula, Leanna, James and Robert. By the time James and Sarah Strickland had migrated to New York with their children, four of my father's first seven children had left home to begin their own families; so they remained in North Carolina.

For several years, there were eleven children in the Long Island household: Beatrice, Samuel, Matthew, Herman, Viola, Arthur, Louvina and I, who were James' and Sarah's eight surviving children; and Roscoe, Cora and Donie who were James' and Gertrude's youngest children. We were a handful, but the family had some great times together. As we grew older, our family's household kept getting smaller and smaller; every year or two, one of my sisters or brothers would get married, leaving home to make a life for themselves.

When I was thirteen years old, our family moved to another little town in Long Island called Mattituck. I completed high school there in three and a half years.

Long Island was a great place to live and raise a family. There was beautiful scenery and the weather was perfect most of the time—except for the hurricanes—the beaches were on both coasts.

I was in three hurricanes on Long Island before I moved into the City. Hurricanes can be very dangerous especially along the Atlantic coast. The first time my brothers, sisters and I were trapped at school. Telephone lines, electric wires and trees were down across the streets; there was debris everywhere and a lot of collapsed buildings. So, they kept us in school all night long until the highway department could clear the streets to make it safe enough where we were able to at least walk.

The next morning I saw my father walking to the school to bring us back home—the school was about two miles from our house in Mattituck. It took over a week before the roads were clear enough to be driven on.

Our barns had been toppled over by the strong winds. We lost some livestock—chickens and pigs, which were killed by the wind and debris. This hurricane happened during the last week of September in 1938.

The next time I was caught in a hurricane, I was on a ferry crossing from Long Island to Branford, Connecticut. Most of the people on board were getting sick because the ferry was riding the big waves up and down. The hurricane lasted more than two hours; all we could do was ride the waves because the ferry could not dock during the storm. If the wind caught the ferry it could have been slammed against the docks and crushed by the turbulence. But we managed to dock as soon as the water was calm enough and calmed down. Everyone was very glad to get off that ferry that day. That was a terrible experience, but thanks to a lot of prayer and a skilled ferry crew, we all managed to survive and arrived safely on shore.

Chapter 6
Me and Uncle Sam

My family moved to another town called Cutchogue, in Long Island. When I was seventeen years old, I did odd jobs and began to work with my family at a duck farm in Riverhead, after school and on weekends. I continued working at the duck farm for two years, with the exception of a brief interval, which commenced on my eighteenth birthday.

During that same time, as soon as I turned eighteen years old, I was called to the service and had been drafted by the army. Because of the immediacy of World War II, the Army's basic training program was little more than a reception process, with basic training lasting just four weeks. But, as fate would have it, I didn't even get through basic training and therefore, never got assigned to active duty. I took the exam and did not pass the physical.

One day during training, I had a severe asthma attack. After that, I was examined and checked every day by the army doctors. The army doctors worked on me trying to clear up my asthma. I remained in camp for about two weeks and was discharged by the doctors after my health improved. I was classified with 4F; the U.S. Army exempted me and I was never called back again. I had asthma on the discharge papers.

When I was called to the army, everybody was very sad. (After all, I was off to the war during very dangerous times.) About nineteen of my family members and friends went to the train station to see me off it and everyone wanted to carry my two bags because they were so sad. They were crying and felt very sorry for me. But then when I was discharged and came back home from the army, very few of my family members were there. It was rather comical. They didn't come back to meet me and help me carry my bags, but they were all glad to see me come back home.

In spite of my ill health, I realized how fortunate I was to have been discharged unharmed. During that war, so many black soldiers died fighting for our country; and still, blacks couldn't get any respect from their fellow-Americans. A few years after my military duty experience, I happened to be in New York City when one of the largest riots in the country broke out.

Chapter 7
Counting My Blessings

Back from basic training, I had returned to the duck farm where my family was working at the time; and I began to get sick again. I knew I'd have to make a change in my occupation.

My asthma had gotten so bad again that, at my doctor's suggestion, my father took me down South to Durham, North Carolina. He had to pay the hospital when I was admitted, even before we knew what the final price would be; this was customary for Blacks who need medical treatment in the South. When we arrived, I was examined and given a few shots of medicine. Then I was checked in at the Three Dukes Hospital, where I stayed for three weeks.

After a series of recommended asthma treatments, and as soon as I was starting to feel better, my doctor released me from the hospital. Of course, that was after the bill was paid. My father and I went back home to Long Island; we traveled both ways by bus.

During the 30's and 40's, there was so much unfair treatment in the hospitals toward Blacks—it's a miracle that any of us who were seriously ill managed to survived. Fortunately, The hospital I stayed in wasn't as bad as the hospital my friend had stayed in a few years earlier. I wanted to share this sad story with you; it has haunted me since I was a little boy.

A good friend of mine was working in a feeding mixer when he slipped and fell into it. The mixer got clogged and jammed, and stopped with him between the blades. When his co-workers untangled him and took him to the hospital, his eyes were bulging out of his head.

At the hospital, my friend was rushed inside through the back door to the only available wing for Blacks; it was one room in the basement with a potbellied stove sitting in the center for heat. My friend lay there unattended for a few days until he died.

That was more than sixty years ago; fortunately, the conditions are changed now. Today, because of many heroic people, blacks are admitted and cared for like any other patients and can be seen in any and all areas of the hospital.

Every day, I count my blessings.

Chapter 8
Learning a Harsh Reality

Back in 1941, after visiting with my relatives in North Carolina for a couple of weeks, I returned to New York very angry about the treatment of coloreds. One day when I was back home thumbing through the newspaper, I became interested in a story that I had read about Keesler Field in Biloxi Mississippi.

I was determined to investigate the Army Base and write a follow-up story, so, during one of my trips to the South, I went to Biloxi, Mississippi. Coincidently, I had heard about a facility there that had special treatments for chronic asthma patients and I wanted to check it out, as well. While I was there in Biloxi, I took the opportunity to visit Keesler Field.

I saw where the white soldiers were staying in better sections of the army barracks than the colored soldiers. I talked to some of the colored soldiers and heard that in order to get merits and qualify for more time off, colored soldiers were asked to clean up the white sections of Keesler Field on their regular days off. And, when they finally did get time off, coloreds would have to go South of the tracks into the poor neighborhoods in order to get a decent meal or have a few drinks; they could not socialize with whites or in the white sections.

If a colored soldier came back home to Mississippi—a dead soldier—he was not allowed to be buried near the white section. I was appalled that, even after dying for their country, the colored soldiers continued to be segregated regardless of their deeds.

There have been many stories told about the heroics of the Tuskegee Airmen; but generally unknown to most was the role that they and other black troops played on Keesler Field.

On June 12, 1941 the War Department had activated Army Air Corps Station No. 8, Aviation Mechanics School, Biloxi, Mississippi. Many of the new recruits stayed at Keesler to become airplane and engine mechanics, while others transferred to aerial gunnery or aviation cadet schools.

In fact, by the autumn of 1943, more than 7,000 Blacks were stationed at Keesler Field. Including: pre-aviation cadets, radio operators, aviation technicians, bombardiers, and aviation mechanics.

Today, Keesler Air Force Base, in Biloxi, Mississippi, is the home of the 81st Training Wing and some of the most invaluable training the Air Force offers new recruits.

Chapter 9
Caught in the Midst of the Harlem Riot

August 1, 1943 was a hot summer night. I was visiting the Apollo Theater in Harlem to see Lena Horne and Cab Calloway performing. While the concert was going on, a riot got started at 125th Street and Lenox Avenue. For our own safety, we were not allowed out of the Apollo until everything calmed down outside.

The Harlem riot had started with an all-too-familiar incident: a white police officer attacking a black soldier. The resulting violence was fed by the anger and frustration that African Americans had faced for centuries. Besides the looting and fires that took place, the 1943 Harlem riot accounted for the deaths of six Harlem men, five at the hands of the police and hundreds of injuries.

The belief that if African Americans proved themselves in fields respected by white Americans, the prejudices that allowed Jim Crow to flourish would dissipate. On the contrary, as proud black soldiers walked around in their uniforms, the gatekeepers of America's racial caste system reacted with growing contempt, and violent clashes between the police and the residents of northern black communities erupted.

The 1943 Harlem riot was a prime example of "enough is enough". I had never seen such a disturbing riot; everything in its path was destroyed. Cars were being overturned, store windows were being broken, and looting was taking place. Jewelry stores, clothing stores, barbershops, gun stores, grocery stores were looted and some were totally destroyed.

The next morning, the looters were selling equipment, jewelry and clothes; at the same time, the city started cleaning up the mess. The streets looked like a tornado had gone through them, with all the debris.

Historically, the 1943 Harlem Riot is referred to as *America's First CommodityRiot.* Unlike earlier race riots, which were battles between white and black Americans, typically begun by whites attacking blacks over some rumored incident, this riot was begun by Harlem residents themselves, and targeted primarily white-owned property in their own neighborhood.

Harlemites, like African Americans everywhere, had gone to war to promote democracy and racial respect at home and abroad. Since World War I, the national civil rights movement had focused on winning economic rights and personal dignity for black service members. While advances were made, such as the election of Adam Clayton Powell Jr. to Common Council, discriminatory practices continued throughout the military. These practices, coupled with the overwhelming number of setbacks and frustrations that blacks continued to endure had resulted in the Harlem riot of August 1, 1943, which represented "one of the many threads that led to the onset of the civil rights movement" a decade later.

Remarking on the destruction wrought during the 1943 Harlem riot, James Baldwin commented, "It would have been better to have left the plate glass as it had been and the goods lying in the stores. It would have been better, but it would also have been intolerable, for Harlem needed something to smash."

Part Two

In whose life will we the difference make,
Are we really willing that chance to take?
Can we through thick and thin be there,
To show someone special we really do care?
For I believe each one of us has a destiny,
A place in life where only we were chosen to be.
But very few are willing to be strong enough,
To stay in this place when the going gets rough.
There may be times our mind is filled with doubt,
And from this place we would like to check out.
Will we press on to fulfill our destiny,
That place in life where only we can be?
Forgetting the pain, not counting the cost,
Even when it seems hopeless and all is lost.
If in just one life a difference I can make,
Then I am willing that chance to take.

—Luckie Haley

Chapter 10
Finding My Soul Mate

One day, while I was in North Carolina for my asthma treatment, I met and fell in love with the young lady that I'm still married to sixty years later—Hazel Roberts. We were both nineteen years old at the time we met—just a few months apart—my birthday is November 3rd and Hazel's is January 2nd.

When I first saw Hazel, I immediately fell in love with her. She was wonderful—warm and soft-spoken, caring and charming—and, so beautiful.

I met her family and they all liked me very much. Whenever I would go over to see Hazel at her house I would stop and spend a lot of time with her dad. Her father would say, "I like that young man" he seems to have something going for him. We would sit out on the front porch and exchange our personal views on life—the way it was and what and how we thought it should be. There needed to be some changes—a lot of changes — especially the way black people were being treated in and out of the schools.

Hazel's brother drove the bus for the school system. He said that when they gave him a bus it was something they didn't want for the white children to ride in, something they had rejected. The bus for the black children broke down a lot because they were not in good shape. Whenever the bus did break down, the driver and the kids would have to wait until the other buses for the white children had finished their route and then he would pick up the remainder of the children to take them home. Sometimes it would be late at night before the black routes were finished and before the black children would get home.

The schools were segregated and, to make matters worse, I couldn't even go to a drugstore and order a coke to drink at the counter. Instead, I would have to go outside of the store to drink it. And, if we wanted to go see a movie, we would have to go to the back of the theater and use the fire escape to go to the top of the building where about twenty or thirty people would be crowded into that area. I remember when the girls would go up the fire escape to the balcony to see a movie and the white boys would stand at the bottom in order to see up their dresses.

Smoking was like a favorite pastime. Just about everybody smoked in North Carolina and Virginia. In the theatre, there was very little ventilation in the attic or balcony for the smoke to go out, so that meant we would have to inhale all that smoke from down below. And, to make matters worse, it wasn't any cheaper in the balcony for blacks; in fact if anything, it was higher.

We didn't go on many dates because I lived in New York and Hazel lived in North Carolina. So, it wasn't easy to communicate, although we did a lot of writing. We courted by mail because phones were not plentiful during that time. Our courtship went on for about a year and a half, and as often as I could, I would be fortunate enough to go down South to visit Hazel.

Hazel lived across the road from my half-sister Leana and her husband Jess Travis, so, when I wanted to visit her, I always had a place to stay. I began traveling back and forth from New York to North Carolina and dated Hazel for about a year and a half. During my travels, I had some memorable experiences, but one long ride still stands out in my mind.

In the South, segregation was really running rampant. I remember one particular trip in 1942 when I was going down south on the Greyhound Bus to visit Hazel. There had been a flood and the bus had to reroute itself to Fayetteville, North Carolina. Because of the flooded streets, the bus driver decided to pull off the road and wait while the passengers all went inside the bus stop restaurant. (Well, almost all.)

The bus stopped right at the front door because it was really raining hard and it was closer to go down the steps and directly inside. But, to my dismay, there was a sign saying, "colored" and an arrow pointing around the back of the restaurant. I didn't want to stir up any unnecessary problems, so I figured that it would be best to follow the instructions. So, I went to the back of the restaurant and saw a window there, measuring about twelve inches by twelve inches, for "colored" people to place their orders.

I stood out there in the pouring rain for about fifteen minutes before a waitress came and took my order for a coke and a hamburger. To make matters worse, the food was priced twice as high at the window for the coloreds as it was inside for the whites. When the waitress finally brought my completed order, it was wrapped in a brown paper sack—she sat it down on the shelf in a puddle of water from the rain—with my coke inside a paper cup that had no lid. I complained to the driver of the Greyhound Bus; but naturally that fell on deaf ears. He said I was lucky to get waited on at all; so you can imagine what the rest of the trip to North Carolina was like.

When I had left New York on the Greyhound, I could sit anywhere on the bus; but as soon as I crossed the Mason Dixon line, I had to take the back seat, sitting on the hard metal benches over the noisy motor of the bus, with nauseating fumes escaping from the motor. *Subconsciously, I guess that trip made me even more determined to marry my sweetheart so she could come back to New York to stay with me.*

I understood that was the way it was all over the South where the blacks were segregated and discriminated against; so I stayed in the South as long as I could and not a moment longer. I was not used to being treated so different—treated like less than a second-class citizen. In New York it was a little better; schools were not segregated and jobs were easier to obtain.

On that trip South, the last one I took before proposing to Hazel, I did a lot of soul searching and I knew a change for the better was coming.

Chapter II
Tying the Knot

While traveling back to New York on that same bus, a gentleman offered me a job working in Brantford, Connecticut at an iron and steel factory, carrying hot ladles of metal (hot steel). At the time, I lived in Long Island and would have to travel by Ferry across the Long Island Sound to work at the steel factory. The salary wasn't the best, but it paid enough to get by—75 cents an hour. I worked there for two summers during the months of July, August and September.

Believe it or not, the summers were cooler inside the factory than they were on the outside. The duck farms were outside and because of the humidity outdoors and the dust, the work there didn't agree with me anyway. I would also be escaping the duck feathers, which contributed to my asthma attacks. The best thing about working at the steel factory was that it would be a step up from my job on the duck farm where I had been working part time, earning 50 cents an hour.

Hazel's father wanted us to move in on his property and build a house but it wasn't my cup of tea to live in the South. In fact, by the time I got back home to New York, I was convinced that I would never live in the South again because of the prejudices towards Blacks—so that's why I decided to ask Hazel to live in New York.

I was ready to pop the question to Hazel, so I asked her to come visit me in New York. During one memorable trip Hazel went to New York to stay with her auntie for about 2 weeks; and while she was there, I proposed to her. She accepted my proposal; we made arrangements and got married—September 3rd, 1944. And, when Hazel drove out to Long Island for the wedding—I was 20 years old and she was 20 years old—just 2 months shy of being 21.

My family's pastor Dr. Reverend John Joseph performed the wedding. Hazel and I drove home with my parents after the wedding, where a small reception followed immediately. For two months, we stayed with my parents until we moved to the Bronx, New York. Hazel and I moved into our own apartment. I got a new job as soon as I got there and settled in.

Chapter 12
To Know Hazel is to Love Hazel

When I met Robuster, I think we were immediately attracted to each other. He was outgoing, fun to be with. He had a good sense of humor, was optimistic about life and kept everyone laughing with his jokes. I liked him very much. He was very convincing that we could become good partners. He was my Mr. Wonderful, so I agreed to marry him.

When Buster left for AZ seeking a better climate for his asthma, I really didn't want to go that far away from my family and neither did he, but we didn't have a choice if he wanted to get some relief. So, wherever he wanted to go, I was going to be there also.

Buster has been a wonderful partner and my best friend. He always wanted the best for our children, and me so he worked hard to provide a good living for us. I am proud to be married to him for 60 years.

Hazel is a very private person, quiet shy and doesn't talk much; but she observes everything.

Hazel could definitely be an interior decorator or a professional seamstress.

Her favorite pastime is working in the yard. She has beautiful flowers and a rose garden and also helps me in my vegetable garden. Hazel and I dine out once or twice a week. We also enjoy going to a movie once in a while and visiting the sick

At one time, she sang in our choir at the First Institutional Baptist Church. When our children were growing up, we took them to church every Sunday and then came home to eat Hazel's traditional fried chicken dinner with all the fixings. Now, after church, she often enjoys spending time with our grandchildren.

Since we've been married, I believe Hazel has only worked two jobs outside of the house. The first was when we lived in New York; she worked in an eyeglass factory polishing eyeglass frames. Later, right after we moved to Arizona, she worked in the Fox Theatre downtown Phoenix.

Once our children started school, Hazel stayed at home to care for them. Rochelle often shares stories about her childhood and especially loves to talk about Hazel. I recently overheard her telling a friend: "My Mother was always there for us. She made sure our homework got done and made sure we did our chores. My Mother is incredible." Hazel was always very involved in school activities; we went to PTA meetings together, but when I couldn't be there she never missed a day.

At the time, I worked two jobs and attended school to further my education, so Hazel often had to be the disciplinarian. She looked after other children in our home, too—I guess in today's terms, it would be called a "Home Day Care". At one time, she took care of as many as eight children– three of them were ours. Hazel has not worked outside of our home since that time.

Marilyn always reminds me of how happy and proud she was when her mother sewed for her. She recalled: "Mother was an excellent seamstress. She made me a yellow and gray checked ruffled dress for my 4th birthday party; I felt like a little princess. I remember one time when my mother made two pin-striped suits—one for herself and one for my father for church." Hazel and I were so sharp in those suits. The first day we wore them to the church, Hazel and I just *knew* that we were the best dress couple in the city.

Hazel always looks good though. She has kept trim and fit by eating well and exercising at least three times a week—either walking a four-mile trek around the Arizona Mills Shopping Mall, or working out at a nearby fitness club.

My son Kenneth refers to Hazel as an angel sent from heaven. He says, "My mother is caring, loving, understanding, supporting, giving, compassionate, affectionate and a spirit-filled servant. She has exemplified strength in the face of adversity, and has always risen to the occasion." I'd say that he has described her up perfectly.

Hazel is an amazing woman! As I have often said, "We have a perfect understanding; she is perfect and I'm understanding." I guess that's part of the glue that has kept us together for 60 years.

Chapter 13
We Are Family

After Hazel and I got married I got a better job delivering bread, cakes and cookies to different stores by van. Hazel also got a job, working at an eyeglass factory part-time. I worked for the bread company for two or three months and we managed to save enough money to move from Long Island to the Bronx.

Once we got situated in the Bronx, I was lucky enough to get a job at the Neighborhood Playhouse for Children in Brooklyn. Things were starting to look better for us in the Bronx—I had a good job and managed to save a little money. Fortunately, I didn't have to own a car because the subway was so cheap— only ten cents and traveled all over the city and then I got a bus pass for just five cents more. So, I rode the subway to work and back for just thirty cents a day; and I could use the company van whenever I needed to transport anything.

Asthma had limited me from participating in sports through my school years or serving in the military; and it had affected my ability to work any jobs requiring strenuous physical involvement. So, I had to change jobs often. But, the job that seemed to agree with me most and the most consistent job I held during that time was as a handyman and a chauffeur— picking up children between the ages of three to six. The Neighborhood Playhouse for Children was school for wealthy children. For five years, I would pick the children up in the morning and take them back home in the evening.

I had been working at the Neighborhood Playhouse for Children when we got a visit from the stork.

Chapter 14
Our First Born

October 2, 1946 our first daughter was born; we named her Marilyn. She would be our only child born in the Bronx, New York.

Marilyn was Daddy's little baby girl—I tried to take her with me everywhere I went. When she was only 2 ½ years old, I began to take Marilyn with me to The Neighborhood Playhouse for Children. Everyone loved her there, so she had the privilege of visiting and participating in the same school that I was driving for. It was a very upscale school and I remember how delighted Marilyn used to be when they served snacks, lunch, milk and crackers in the afternoon.

We enjoyed spending time with our little daughter Marilyn—especially during the Spring, Summer and Fall months. She would love to see the animals and birds at the zoo. We would all go to the movies, museums, concerts, parks, Coney Island, the Empire State Building and to visit family and friends in the different boroughs.

Even at such a young age, Marilyn loved the city life. But it was quite a tiring trip for as young as she was, to travel back and forth several times a month. The Winters were especially rough and damp; and it snowed a lot. In fact, I would see snow on the ground, sometimes, all winter long, for three months at a time. This made transportation almost impossible, except for the city buses and subways. Living in the city was a lot different than it had been in the country—out on Long Island.

Chapter 15
The Long Commute

So, for five years, we had been living in the Bronx and I had been riding the subway from the Bronx to Brooklyn—it took about an hour to get to work and then about an hour to get back home on the subway. My boss, Harold Lewis, and I hit it off really well, but unfortunately, it could not continue. I felt my asthma getting worse; my health was failing.

After a while, getting around in New York was becoming very challenging. As Hazel and I did not yet have our own car, commuting to work, as well as socially was becoming more and more of a major task. For example, when Hazel and I were growing up, both our families had instilled in us a strong faith in God; and we tried to instill that same faith in our new little family. So, most Sundays, we took the subway from the Bronx to Harlem to attend the Abyssinian Baptist Church, where the Reverend Adam Clayton Powell was pastor.

While we lived in the Bronx, Hazel and I would also take a train from the Bronx to visit my family—my father, mother, first 3 sisters and 4 brothers—every month, which was about 85 miles out on the Island (Long Island). Of course, the best way to get out to Long Island from where we were living in the Bronx, was to take a train.

The physical attributes of commuting were beginning to take a toll on my health. Little did I know, my life would soon change drastically.

Chapter 16
Gaining A New Lease On Life

In the fall of 1949, in my 5th year of working at The Neighborhood Playhouse for Children, my asthma was really giving me trouble breathing. But, I worked without a break, right up until I had to go to the Lebanon Hospital in the Bronx with a really bad asthma attack. The doctor treated my asthma, and, after seeing my weak condition he admitted me immediately. What I thought was just another asthma attack was diagnosed as a near fatal condition of double pneumonia. I didn't realize it at the time, but my health was fading very rapidly—I weighed only 117 pounds.

For three weeks, I had to stay in the hospital in a portable oxygen tent. I had two doctors who suggested that I should leave New York and go to Arizona because the climate was dry there; even though they believed it was too late to save my life. In fact, both doctors gave me just a year to live in Arizona and less than a year to live if I stayed in New York. That was nearly sixty years ago.

I had asthma so bad that the doctors insisted on putting me right on the plane straight from the hospital without returning back home to my apartment in the Bronx. My brave young wife, Hazel made all the arrangements to send me to Arizona by plane.

The trip was very trying for me; I was weak and breathing was difficult. I was relieved to reach my final destination. It was an eight-hour flight on American Airlines; the plane stopped in Oklahoma and all the passengers were required to change to another plane to finish the trip to Phoenix.

This wasn't the first time a doctor had given me such a dismal diagnosis, and once again my strong faith in God led me to believe that I could beat the odds. At the time, I knew that I had a special purpose on this earth and I was determined to discover it and to nurture it.

Chapter 17

Me and My Guitar

I never played the guitar professionally, but I always admired guitar music. It is my favorite musical instrument and it was my first musical instrument.

When I was a child, I used to admire my older brother Roscoe's guitar. Roscoe didn't live with us, but whenever we went to visit him, he would let me play it. I was so excited about that guitar that I just couldn't stop talking about it. Finally, one Christmas, my mother and father must have decided it was time for me to get the gift I wanted so badly. When I peeked in the closet on Christmas Eve and saw the guitar handle sticking up, I was so excited I couldn't sleep. Before dawn, I awoke my brothers and sisters and led the crew into the living room. I ran over to "my" guitar and read the tag; much to my dismay, it said "Samuel, Matthew, Herman and Robuster". I couldn't believe that I had to share it with my older brothers.

The plan was that we would each have the guitar all to ourselves one week out of the month. But, it turned out that they weren't really interested in playing the guitar, so they worked out a deal with me to trade for guitar time. I would do each brother's chores the week he had the guitar and he would repay me by letting me use it in his place. This turned out to be my first lesson in "economics"—I was so happy. I kept that guitar until I was sixteen years old.

I enjoyed playing the guitar for my own satisfaction, although, I play mostly by ear. When Hazel and I were living in the Bronx, she loved to hear me play. I bought a new guitar and took lessons for about a year and a half in Greenwich Village.

The world-renowned baritone singer Paul Roberson was one of my teachers; it was one of the most-fulfilling experiences I ever had.

It's interesting that my first lesson in economics came from bartering for a guitar; and I never considered the significance that would continue to play in my life. When the need arose, I sold my new guitar for $150 to help finance my move to Phoenix; it was quite a deal considering I had bought it for just $20. With the money from my guitar, $50 that my brother Roscoe gave me, and many blessings from God and my family, I would never look back. I managed to save my life, build a new life and live my life to its fullest.

I guess I could honestly say that guitar music is my passion. I really love the guitar; even seventy years after holding one for the first time, I still strum on it for relaxation and for serenading Hazel and my friends.

Since I moved to Phoenix, I have actually bought four other guitars. From 1970 to 1971 I took guitar lessons from Ziggy's Music Studio on Central and Washington Streets in Phoenix—about five miles from where I lived. To this day, I regret that, I didn't continue with those lessons. Every now and then, in my spare time, I still pick up my guitar and play it.

Part Three

If these walls could talk
They would speak of a man
Who has worked with great heart
To accomplish his plan.
They'd speak of the times
That he's prayed in the Night
For the strength to go on
And to do what is right
They'd speak of sweet moments
Of laughter and fun
The times with his children
His love for each one
Oh, if they could talk
It would just be the start
Of a story of love,
a great man and his heart

Chapter 18
Arizona Here I Come!

I arrived in Phoenix, Arizona September 2nd 1949—the temperature was 102. On the contrary, when I left New York it had been 40 degrees. Upon my arrival in Phoenix, as soon as I got off the plane, I saw a *brother*! I'll never forget J.D. Holmes; he was a caring and concerned young man. To this day, I don't know why he was at the airport; but I sure thanked God for leading him there.

I asked Mr. Holmes where the Black area of Phoenix was located and if he knew where I could get a place to stay. Without hesitating, he took me to the Hackett Inn, the only Black Hotel in Phoenix. He had told me that this hotel was the only one in town for "coloreds". So, I rented a room and stayed there for a few days, after which I graciously accepted an invitation to stay at his in-laws' home for a month.

When I arrived in Phoenix, I was weighing in at 117, until I started getting my health back. Funny, I had always wanted to weigh 150 pounds, but I never saw that at all....I just went right on past it.

Getting established in a new place is never easy, but I attribute much of my success to the young man who took me by the hand when I got off the plane in Arizona. I began my journey there surrounded by a small village of black men and women who refused to settle for second best.

Years later, in 1963, that same young man who took me by the hand would open more doors for our community. J.D. Holmes, along with two other "Negroes"(as we were called then)—Leon Thompson and

Cloves C. Campbell, Sr.—would be elected to the Arizona's Twenty-Sixth Legislature of the House of Representatives.

Arizona turned out to be a good move for my family and for the thousands of the African-American families who migrated here for health reasons or just for a lifestyle change. In January 1967, Mr. Campbell was sworn into the State Senate of Arizona under the 28th State Legislature, as the first "Negro" in Arizona to achieve this honor. Many other African-American political leaders, including: the Honorable Calvin Goode, Cody Williams and Michael Johnson would span decades as City Council Members; and the Arizona Informant (newspaper) would keep us in the know.

Today, I am a close friend to Calvin Goode who has prepared my taxes for over 30 years; and I have known Michael Johnson and Cody Williams since they were babies.

I am truly grateful that God led me to J.D. Holmes when I first arrived in Arizona in 1949. He was very instrumental in helping me get started when I moved here; he was a brother in Christ and a very good friend. J.D. Holmes passed away recently

Chapter 19
There's No Place Like Home

Hazel and Marilyn had come out to Phoenix on the train in October 1949—two months after I arrived there. We stayed in the rented room for a few months and saved up enough money to buy a home right around the corner.

Segregation was so bad in Phoenix that the only area that was available for blacks to purchase property was in the south of the river bottom between 24th and 16th Streets in 1949. So, that's where we began…. and where we raised our family…. and where we lived for nearly four decades.

The first home we bought was just newly built at 4417 S 18th Place in Phoenix, Arizona. A two-bedroom house cost us $5280 in 1949 and it was at the payment of $150 down and $27.50 a month; and we had to have a co-signer with good credit before we could qualify to buy a home at that price in South Phoenix. We bought the home and added rooms and improved on the property—the family thoroughly enjoyed the new swimming pool and heated covered spa.

When I arrived in Arizona, because of my asthma, I received all kinds of advice. Someone, in fact, said that bees would extract pollen from the things I was allergic to; and that would help me build up my immune system. *Actually, in a single day, one bee makes 12 or more trips from the hive, visiting several thousand flowers.* So, I tried that for a few years. I had many bees; and a lot of honey.

I started with one queen bee, which I got from Indiana. I was told that was where I could get the queen bee that I wanted—so they shipped it here along with a few others, drones. When I brought the bees to Arizona, I just put them into a box; eventually I had seven or eight different boxes. From there on, the bees just multiplied.

I hired a beekeeper and he would come in and smoke them. My beekeeper would put on his little mask and get the honey out of the honeycombs—the bees were all over him. It was a lot of work. I was afraid of the bees; but they stayed in their boxes and never stung me.

I kept bees for 2 or 3 years, but I stopped because one stung Marilyn. Her whole arm was in a cast all the way to her shoulder. We were very frightened, so I had to get rid of the bees.

Chapter 20
How Does Your Garden Grow?

A few years after we bought our home, the empty lot next door became available; we bought it so we could expand our backyard. The lot was 90 by 128 feet; my plan was to cultivate it and turn it into a garden. To my dismay, the soil was infertile, so you couldn't grow anything on it; but I wasn't going to let that stop me. I had grown up farming, was still a farmer at heart, and I loved my gardens.

The soil had to be treated, so I changed it by adding two hundred and fifty tons of treated soil, and mixed it in with lots of mulch. After digging and mixing the soil, it was very good for planting and raising vegetables and fruit.

By the time I had finished, I had grown a full garden of vegetables, including: squash, green beans, collard greens, onions, potatoes and even tobacco. I raised more than enough for my family and an abundance of prepared and canned fruit and vegetables to last us after the season was over. In fact, we even supplied vegetables and fruit for the entire neighborhood.

My garden grew magnificently, so I began to participate in several local contests. The first year, I entered a vegetable contest and took first place for the largest squash—the next year I entered a tobacco plant, which was ten feet high; it got first place. I was told that ten feet was a record in Arizona.

The tobacco plant was very interesting to most people and drew much attention; a lot of folks had never seen a tobacco plant and they were coming from all over the valley to see how it was grown. There were three or four older men in the area, which used tobacco, so I didn't have any trouble getting rid of the leaves—they smoked it and chewed it.

There are two different planting times—in the spring and fall, so it was not very long between seasons. I couldn't take care of the garden alone, so I had young men in the area help me take care of it, which also helped keep kids out of the streets and earn a little extra money. I also shared the fruit and vegetables from my garden with them and it helped their families.

At one point, I had become so excited about growing my own food again, that I got a few ducks chickens and a lamb; and I turned my garden into a small farm. The entire farming experience was very enriching and educational for our family and friends and it helped me stay connected to my roots.

After we moved to Awhatukee from South Phoenix, I missed my little farm.

Chapter 21
Everything Must Change

There were poisonous snakes and insects in the area; but we learned that they were common throughout the state of Arizona. Sometimes when we would come back from dinner or the drive-in movies, we would have to take the flashlight and go through the entire house to look for scorpions and spiders in the house. They even climbed under the sheets or hid in our slippers and shoes. I remember one time when Marilyn found a scorpion under her rug by the bed. I even found a Gila monster once in our front yard and caught it in a cage.

The streets were non-existent. Broadway, which was the main street running through our part of town, was a little dirt road with no pavement—just a narrow cement pathway for two cars to pass. Bus service was limited and ran, probably every two hours.

We lived about a mile away from the Salt River. In November 1973, however, the Salt River was running swiftly from one bank to the other. This happened especially in the spring when it rained heavily. The water came down to the river when the snow melted way up in the mountains. It pushed the rain off into the River and we'd see water as high as the Central Avenue Bridge, often running over the top of the bridge.

There was the only way to cross from the South side of Phoenix to the North side. Whenever this happened, it was a huge disadvantage for all those that had to go to work or to get to the doctor, the hospitals or other businesses on the other side of the River. The largest river run lasted for two weeks and most of the people affected by this flood were South of the river. …and most minorities were living South of the river.

In 1982 several new bridges were built across the Salt River at 7th St, 16th St. 24th St. and 7th Avenue and a few other places to accommodate the people living South of the river. It's hard to believe it, but the entire river that once ran through South Central Phoenix is completely dried up now.

My second and third children Rochelle and Kenneth were born while we were living at 4417 South 18th Place. All three of my children went to the predominantly Black grammar school in South Phoenix. They graduated from the nearby South Mountain High School and attended college in Phoenix.

We lived on South 18th Place for thirty-eight years, until March 1988. By then, the area was growing and beginning to look decent enough to live in—Broadway was even paved. But, the children were grown and gone; so Hazel and I decided to move on. We built our second house in Ahwatukee (a newly developed suburb of Phoenix) where we live today.

Today, when I visit the old neighborhood, I see phenomenal changes. New schools have been built, and as in most urban communities that may have been gentrified, South Phoenix is undergoing the change. The streets where my children grew up, which are just 10 minutes from the America West Arena and the Bank One Ballpark have become entwined with new developments. New homes are selling upwards of $180,000.00 because of their proximity to the Sky Harbor Airport and Downtown Phoenix or their breathtaking mountain views or city skylines.

I'm glad we moved on when we did. Our children had grown and we wanted a change of scenery. Hazel and I both have our gardens—I plant vegetables and she plants flowers. We don't have a pool anymore, but we enjoy our relaxing hot tub nestled in our beautiful spacious landscaped yard. And, we're in close proximity from Sky Harbor Airport and just minutes away from the place that would play a significant role in my life's journey.

Our Family Album

Hazel Roberts Strickland in 1952, taken in Phoenix, AZ, age 27

Robuster, Kenneth and Rochelle showing off their catch for the day – Phoenix, AZ

Rochelle, Kenneth and cousin taken in Ararat, VA – visiting from Phoenix, AZ

*Two beauties – Hazel and my sister
Beatrice strike a pose*

Robuster and Hazel, our home

*Our stairsteps – Marilyn, Rochelle
and Kenneth*

*Buster showing off another catch of
the day*

Marilyn Strickland at a piano recital, Julian School, Phoenix, AZ

Hazel's sister Pearl with little Marilyn

Marilyn Strickland, daughter, School Picture – 1956

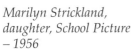

Our home on 18th Place, Phoenix, AZ – Hazel, Marilyn, Rochelle and Kenneth, Buster's brother: Arthur, Wife and Baby

Hazel, Marilyn, teacher and friend at charm and grace school for children (1951), Phoenix, AZ

61

Little Marilyn, 3 years old

Hazel Strickland, Easter Sunday at home in Phoenix, AZ (1962)

TEEN OF THE WEEK

Marilyn Strickland, 17, South Mountain High School senior, is the Arizona Tribune Teen of the Week.

She leads a busy life while maintaining her scholastic average. As a former Pom Pom girl, she was seen at most of the sport activities last year. She is a member of the Future Business Leaders of America, NAACP and First Institutional Baptist Church.

Marilyn plans to attend Arizona State University and major in business administration.

She is the daughter of Mr. and Mrs. Robuster Strickland, 4417 S. 18 Place.

Marilyn, 17 years, South Mountain High School Senior AZ Tribune teen of the week, a former pom pom girl Phoenix, AZ (1965)

Tamra – my first granddaughter – Phoenix, AZ

Friends, Ira McNear and Mr. O'Neil taken in my back yard (Phoenix, AZ 1984) Tobacco plant I grew – took first place ever in AZ

Robuster and a squash that won first place at the state fair 1984 – Picture taken at our home, 4417 S. 18th Place.

Hazel admiring Buster's Squash

Ducks Buster raised in backyard

Our home, backyard: Buster, Hazel and friends from Long Island, NY

Buster with more fish

Our house at 4417 S. 18th Place, Phoenix, AZ where we took our swimming lessons with some of our friends

Hazel & Robuster – at home in Phoenix – showing off his fish 4417 South 18th Place

Buster at home showing off his catch of the day

Buster's catch

Buster's promotion to analyst at Sky Harbor Airport

AIRPORT OPERATION ANALYST — Pointing to a study area is Robuster Strickland, recently promoted analyst. He was assigned to conduct planning and control systems at Phoenix' Sky Harbor International Airport. He has been a city employee for 10 years.

Buster at work with coworker Amillio Reyes, City of Phoenix

Buster at a dance recital

Buster and his dance instructor at a recital at Arthur Murray's Dance Studio

Kenneth Strickland and son Matthew at our 75th birthday party–Phoenix, AZ 1999

Anthony Strickland (Buster's grandson) with his son Anthony Jr. (Buster's great grandson)

Jason Livingston (Buster's grandson) and daughter Jaleigh (Buster's great granddaughter)

Rochelle & Robuster having a chat

Rochelle & Nate's wedding and reception at our house – 1986

Judge takes over top job in 'fantasyland

By VENITA HAWTHORNE JAMES
Arizona Republic Staff

When Cecil B. Patterson Jr. worked after school in his father's laundry in Virginia, there were always people big on the bottle and down on their luck coming around asking for food or clothing.

Nowadays, he still sees a lot of people with problems, but he's a little more removed from them — about 2 feet up, on a Maricopa County Superior Court bench.

Today, he becomes presiding criminal judge, overseeing 12 other judges. He'll shift roles from an active judge to an administrator, although he'll still try a few cases.

Patterson replaces John Seidel, who moves to the civil division.

"I'm not unmindful of the magnitude of the job," says Patterson, 44, who was appointed a judge in 1980. He welcomes the challenge.

But it will be different from the past five years.

* * *

One day in court last week, Patterson quietly questioned a defendant he was about to sentence.

"Did you finish school?" Patterson asked.

"Yes, sir," the man answered.

Patterson looked approving.

Later in his office, the judge said, "I have a very high regard for education. It's one thing I'll get very conservative on, get very hard and nasty. I know what it's done for me and my family. It's allowed me to send my daughter to a first-rate university and to buy myself a shirt now and then."

He says that that's why, two or three times a week, he makes earning the equivalent of a high school diploma a part of the sentences he hands out.

In the five years since he became a judge, Patterson, a tall man with graying sideburns, has become known as a judge who tries to be fair.

George Logan, an assistant director for the state Department of Economic Security, says the legal community regards Patterson as serious, hard-working and knowledgeable about law.

"He's not considered to be some legal genius who writes treatises for everyone to read," Logan says. "But he will educate himself and

— *Judge, B3*

Peter Schuster/Rep.

Cecil Patterson reviews his agenda with secretary Rochelle Mill

Rochelle on the job with her boss Cecil Patterson (she was his secretary)

Buster with grandson Anthony Strickland

Buster's grandchildren Anthony Strickland & Christine Lawson – Easter Sunday in Arizona

Buster and great granddaughter Alexis

Buster's grandaughter Tamra and great granddaughter Tameka at home.

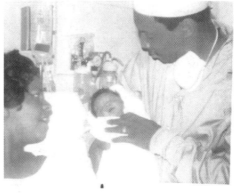

My daughter Marilyn Livingston with her husband George during the birth of their son Jason – in California

Grandson Anthony Strickland geared up to play football for his school team

My great granddaughter Alexis

Grandson Jason Livingston riding a horse at McDonald Ranch

Kenneth, Hazel, Rochelle, Buster , Marilyn at Rochelle's wedding (first marriage)

Buster & Yvonne at Camelback Mountain, Scottsdale, AZ

Niece of hazel's and Hazel's dad, Buster and Grandson Anthony visiting in California 1976

Niece, Yvonne, my grandchildren & Hazel – Scotsdale, AZ

Buster and Hazel on Starward Cruise Ship, Norwegian Lines in Caribbean, 7 days

Norwegian Caribbean Lines NCL **First fleet of the Caribbean.**   M S Starward

Buster, Eula Heard, Hazel and Dave Heard on a Caribbean cruise .

Hazel and her girlfriends strike a pose in front of the cruiseship.

73

Hazel & Buster's great nephew Curtis in the backyard

Hazel & Buster vacationing in Colorado

Marilyn, Buster's great nephew Curtis, his wife Alexis, and Hazel at our home – my nephew was visiting from Chicago – 2004

Hazel, Tamra, Marilyn, Tameka at Tamra's wedding – October 26, 2000

Robuster and Tamra Strickland at Tamra's Wedding – Buster gave her away in Phoenix, AZ (2000)

Buster & Hazel at Grandaughter Tamra's wedding

Nate & Rochelle at Tamra's wedding

Our 50th Wedding Anniversary at Val Vista Estates in Gilbert, AZ 1994

Buster and Hazel, 75th Birthday Party, 1999

The marriage ministry at 1st Institutional Baptist Church, Rev. Warren Stewart, Hazel & Robuster – they received a plaque for being married for 60 years

Rochelle, Hazel, Buster, Kenneth and Marilyn, Buster's birthday at home

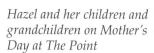

Hazel and her children and grandchildren on Mother's Day at The Point

Party for Richard Nixon at Barry Goldwater's home

*Kenneth , Buster, Fife Symington, Bob & Friend at Fife's home
during his open house –2004*

Wedding reception for Barry Goldwater

Buster & Hazel entertaining friends at their home in Ahwatukee, AZ

Buster and family just after winning the Wheel of Fortune Jackpot at Gila River Casino

Kenneth & Buster celebrating in Las Vegas (1998) after Buster hit the million-dollar jackpot at the Gila River Casino in Phoenix.

The winning machine

Buster celebrating his 81st birthday with family (front) Kenneth, Marilyn, Buster, Hazel, Rochelle (back) Tameka, Tamra, Alexis & Kristine

Buster and Tameka at Buster's 81st birthday party

Chapter 22
Marilyn Jean Strickland

When I was three years old my mother and I rode the train from New York to Phoenix. Because of his critical asthma condition, my father had come to Phoenix from New York by plane one month before we arrived. Dad's doctors had only given him a few months to live, if he did not relocate. They thought the Phoenix climate would be his last hope. Because my father does not meet a stranger, he met friends easily and quickly in Phoenix and accepted his new path in life head on.

—Marilyn

Marilyn had just turned three years old when she and Hazel came to Phoenix in October 1949.

Marilyn's childhood was filled with expectations of excelling; she really liked school. Marilyn received awards in typing skills, shorthand skills, FBLA (Future Business Leaders of America). She took piano lessons every Saturday morning at Ms. McMahon's house from the time she was six years old. She did not really enjoy it then, but she now realizes the importance of discipline and how important it is to be focused.

Marilyn made me so proud when she took over some of her instructor's students. Although she was a shy kid, she was in major roles in plays in elementary school, piano recitals, baton twirling, parades and dance classes.

At the end of her freshman year, she tried out for the Varsity Pom Pom Squad and made it! She was on the Varsity Team during her sophomore and junior years. If it weren't for that, she would not have been able to attend all the football games, basketball games and track events, as well as going to Tucson for a game.

When she was a freshman in High School at South Mountain High school, she was asked to the senior prom by the president of the student body, who also happened to be the Captain of the football team—with a 4.0 average. Of course, since she was a freshman, his father had to accompany them to the Senior Prom, wait for them and escort them to a Chinese restaurant afterwards and back home. This was quite a relief to me.

Marilyn attended other school proms with other students of the community, as well. She went to her own senior prom with her (unbeknownst to us) future husband. Marilyn looked so beautiful that night. Hazel made her a sky blue prom dress and her date wore a blue tuxedo.

Marilyn had pneumonia during the eighth grade and missed a lot of school right before graduation. She graduated with her class but did not actually receive a Diploma until she made up some classes that summer.

Marilyn went to college at Phoenix College at the age of seventeen years old. She majored in Business Administration. Because of her excellent business skills, she attained many positions at an early age, administering over employees much older than herself. Always the enterprising young lady, when she was in college, Marilyn played the piano at the Arizona State University Chapel during her lunch hour to earn money for the summer.

Marilyn met her first husband in Arizona State University when he was on a football scholarship from Pennsylvania in 1964 and got married in 1966.

Marilyn Jean Strickland (Livingston) gave birth to three children: Tamra, born January 4, 1966; Kristine, born April 16, 1969 and Jason Robuster Livingston (deceased), born May 26, 1976. Marilyn also has three granddaughters: Tameka Shante Flowers—daughter of Tamra, born April 30, 1983; Alexis Mohr—daughter of Kristine, born May 17, 1992 and Jaleah Livingston—daughter of Jason, born May 5, 1998.

Marilyn has worked as an executive assistant in various private and public sectors for more than last forty years. She was a courtroom clerk in the late 60's for the Superior Court of Maricopa County; a secretary for various governmental agencies in Phoenix and Toronto, Ontario, Canada;

Secretary to the Director of Research at University Hospital in Seattle, Washington; Secretary to the President of the Arizona State Senate, President Leo Corbet, as well as other senators after his term.

Marilyn took an early retirement in 2002 years ago, shortly after her son Jason's murder, which happened during a carjacking in South Phoenix. The devastation of my grandson's death was magnified by the fact that it occurred on my birthday November 4, 2001, an event, which we had customarily celebrated my birth each year. Now, we also celebrate Jason's life on November 4th and remember it as the day that Jason was "called home" by the Lord.

Chapter 23
Rochelle Aloise Strickland (Hawthorne)

My father influenced me in fishing from a very young age and gardening a few years ago.

Fishing was probably one of my favorite things that I enjoyed with him. I still enjoy the sport and he enjoys it so much that just watching him brings me so much joy. Many times I would go fishing with my father by myself and that gave me great pleasure because I loved to talk to him; it seemed to bring us closer. My father is a very compassionate man. Besides being there consistently for his family, he visits the sick and shut in on a regular basis...always helping others.

—Rochelle

Our second child, Rochelle was born December 2, 1951. Rochelle has one natural child, Anthony Charles Strickland, born April 11, 1971 and one grandson Anthony Janais Strickland born march 19, 2001. She also has three step-children, Victor Hawthorne, age 34, Natasha Wilson, Age 33 and Natalie Hawthorne, age 28 and three step grandchildren—Tylan Hawthorn, age 15 and a set of twins Kyle and Kennedy Hawthorne, age 3.

Rochelle is on medical disability. Much of her career has been spent in the legal field. She retired from the criminal justice system in the year 2000 where she had been working as a judicial assistant for Cecil B. Patterson, Jr., an Appellant Court Judge, for nineteen years. Rochelle had worked for Mr. Patterson when he was at the Superior Court level and, prior to that, she worked as his administrative assistant while he was a practicing attorney.

Rochelle was a sweet girl—she loved Hazel and me very much. She had me wrapped around her little finger, though, and just knew she could get away with more from me than she could from her mother.

Rochelle loved to read and she liked it very much when Hazel read to her. She read several books when she was a child. Her teachers told her how good she was in spelling, so she really worked on it. She began entering spelling bees and when she started winning them it gave her the motivation to keep studying. To this day, Rochelle remembers a spelling bee contest that she lost when she was in the 5th grade competing with a 9th grader. Rochelle had beaten everyone else; she was getting tired and nervous and the last word was "candle". All of a sudden she couldn't see the word to save her life and she spelled it "candel". As soon as she did, she knew it was not the right way. She will never forget that, and I will never forget her disappointment and pain.

Rochelle was very outgoing and loved to be involved with her brother and sister in various activities. Hazel and I started sending Rochelle to take piano lessons. I think mainly she wanted to go because her older sister Marilyn was going. She often reminds me of how proud she felt when she and Marilyn were in their recitals, and we would be in the audience taking pictures. Rochelle took piano lessons for years.

When Marilyn started taking baton lessons, so she could be in a baton club, Rochelle had to do this also. Hazel and I were always there with the children, taking pictures and showing our support. Rochelle and he brother Kenneth even had go-carts, which they competed with at the track.

Rochelle is married to a wonderful man, Nate Hawthorne.

Chapter 24
Kenneth Leon Strickland

My Dad is a workaholic and a provider; but he is also gentle, caring and fun loving. I remember fondly the many times we have gone fishing. Once, when I was a child, we were on a fishing trip and he made me believe I had caught a big fish, when my line was tangled up with his. We still laugh about it.

When I was a teenager, my dad bought me a go-kart that I would race at the Fair grounds. But, when I started my own business, I did not have time to continue the sport. . At an early age he taught me that hard work was necessary to become successful in life. My dad was the influence behind my catering business.

Thank you for a job well done! Daddy congratulations on your book and mother keep on believing and living, going and growing, sharing and caring as an active witness for the Kingdom of God.

—Kenneth

Our third child Kenneth Leon Strickland was born at St. Joseph's Hospital in Phoenix, Arizona on August 23, 1955. Kenneth has one son, named Matthew Cordell Strickland, who was born October 10, 1987.

Kenneth often remarks about his childhood being filled with memories of family gatherings, friends and church. We would attend church on a regular basis, so he was introduced to religion at a very young age. Kenneth enjoyed singing in the children's choir, attending bible school and participating in various functions held at church.

Kenneth started playing little league baseball at nine years old. By the time he reached Junior High, he played basketball, football and had started bowling. When Kenneth was eleven years old, I bought him a go-kart that he would race at the Fair grounds. A few years later, Kenneth bought his first car from me with the money he had saved from a part time landscaping job that he and I did together. Shortly after that, he became interested in dating, but rarely had time due to his job responsibilities.

I was very proud of Kenneth when he graduated early from South Mountain High School in January 1973. After graduation, he started working for the City of Phoenix engineering department, where he was employed for twelve years. During that time, Kenneth played American Legion Baseball for the City of Phoenix for two years and received a promotion on his job.

While working for the City of Phoenix, Kenneth sought out avenues for advancements, so he started taking classes at Phoenix College and Mesa Community College. His progress was slowed down for a while when he experienced difficulty dealing with peer pressure and making the right choices.

Now Kenneth is the owner of a thriving business, A-Team Catering, Inc., which has been in operation since 1995. He had become owner/partner with me in the family business in 1977 (Ken's Contract Catering) and when I retired, Kenneth began the existing company.

Kenneth often says that I'm a workaholic and a provider. Ironically, he has chosen to follow in my footsteps.

Chapter 25
Driving Ms. McKay

One of my first jobs that I had when I got to Phoenix was working as a driver for a lady named Mrs. McKay—a very wealthy lady. The funny thing was that she never went out without her dog—and while she rode in the back seat, he always rode up front with me. As the driver, it was my responsibility to keep the car nice and shiny and that dog used to hang his head out the window and slobber all over the side of the car. It was so frustrating to clean up after him every time he rode in the front.

One day Ms. McKay didn't feel well but she still wanted me to drive her dog around. Of course, it upset me, but it was my job, so I did it. Well… she thought I did it. I put the dog in the car and drove him straight to my apartment, picked up my wife and baby and drove them around for two hours—I left the dog at home. When I went back to get him he was so happy to jump into the car and after he got home, he was extra jubilant.

Ms. McKay was so pleased by her dog's excitement to be home. I worked for her for two months—she liked me and she liked my driving. But, she wanted all her help to be "light-skinned" and never accepted Hazel because she was "brown-skinned".

After a while I grew tired of her criticisms about my wife. Finally, I quit my job, and Ms. McKay and her attorney begged me to come back—they even told me that I was in her will. Well, as far as I was concerned, it didn't matter, not as much as my family. Ms. McKay died two years later, and I guess I'll always wonder—*how much?*

Chapter 26
Bringing Home the Bread

After I left my job driving Ms. McKay, another opportunity opened up. This time I was be able to enjoy Hazel's company full time because we worked together in our own business. We were even able to bring our little girl Marilyn along with us; and Hazel was expecting our second daughter Rochelle.

Banner Bakery was losing sales because they didn't have any drivers in the Black communities; there were no bakery services on the South Side or West Side areas of Phoenix. At that time, they were willing to try anything to get things up and running. They found me by word of mouth; and I was given an opportunity to get into the bakery business.

In the early 1950's, there weren't a lot of supermarkets and most people had to walk a distance to the small community stores. Banner Bakery had started a special service bringing bread directly to the people. I was assigned certain areas where there was a lack of service and would deliver to the stores there as well as to private homes in the Black communities. My task was to deliver all kinds of "fresh" baked goods—pies, cakes, pastries and bread.

I bought a bread truck from the bakery, under contract, and made monthly payments on it. In addition, it was my responsibility to keep my truck serviced and filled with gas.

Every morning except Sunday, I went to the bakery, loaded up my truck with baked goods and went door to door in my designated areas. My customers would select fresh bakery supplies two different times a week at their doorstep. In areas where the houses were close together, Hazel would drive the truck from door to door (that's how she learned to drive stick shift) while I walked along, sold and delivered the baked goods. This happened five days a week, Monday through Friday. On Saturday, I just delivered the goods that had been previously ordered; that way almost everything we had was sold and very little was left on the truck to be absorbed by me. I had to use the leftovers or lose money on the remainder; so, on occasion, I would either give baked goods to my neighbors or donate them to charitable organizations.

I received 33 1/3% of all my sales and paid the balance to Banner Bread. They would take my truck payments and their overhead out of the money that I turned in. It was a good business for me because I loved meeting people and I had Hazel to keep the orders straight and balance the books.

I worked for the bakery, under contract, for six months; and generated enough business to purchase a second truck, hire a driver and begin another route. In less than a year, I had built a thriving business. Unfortunately, all that changed much too soon; I began to see the bakery department business going down and the Banner Bread ultimately declared bankruptcy. At the request of the owner, I stayed on for a couple of months after my contract was up; and I was reimbursed for whatever payments I made on my trucks.

My work with Banner Bread helped me learn my way around the city; I had the opportunity to visit many communities. I'm certain that this experience helped me to get hired by the Maricopa County Highway Department in Phoenix.

Chapter 27
Segregation Loomed All Around Us

In the 1950's while we lived in Phoenix, Arizona, Hazel, the children and I made two trips back to New York to visit our families by car—two very educational trips for the kids, and for us, as well. Segregation was very much in full-force; and we experienced it extensively while we were traveling. The hotels, restaurants, restrooms and recreational areas where we could stop along the way were marked specifically for "coloreds" and most of the facilities charged us higher prices to use their services.

Segregation in Phoenix was really widespread, too—especially in jobs, restaurants, shows, and so forth. The Fox Theatre where we would go had a special section for colored viewers.

On the job segregation and discrimination was also very common. I put in an application in Maricopa County Highway Department to work—driving a truck. I became the first black truck driver for the Maricopa County Highway Department in Phoenix. It was the only decent job that was being offered to blacks, at the time; that was an experience. They gave me a condemned truck to drive.

On this particular job, the man who drove the loader, that loads on sand and rock, loaded my truck up with as much as he could put on it—he even had it all over the cab. I didn't complain—I just drove the truck onto the street and the front wheels spread out and emptied the load right on 19th Ave. The man who loaded my truck got reprimanded and almost lost his job. The county supervisor then bargained with me and was eager to please me. He gave me another truck because he thought that if I pursued it, he would have a legal case on his hands. But, instead, I held that job down for 10 years.

When I heard that City of Phoenix needed a truck driver, I saw it as an opportunity to advance. I took the exam and was hired. I started with the city of Phoenix driving a garbage/trash truck; and learned that I was their "first" colored driver. I got in with the other drivers, but, of course being the only colored driver, I experienced a lot of racism. However, I always looked for ways to improve, so whenever possible, I took classes.

I drove a trash truck during the day and, whenever I could, went to school at night. I didn't earn any degrees, but I took different classes and studies where I wanted to excel. For instance, I felt that a class in Spanish was essential. I could see the necessity of speaking Spanish.... especially with the Spanish-speaking people. So, I studied Spanish, English 101, Inspections, Management Analyst, Inspector's Chief and Inspector of Streets & Sanitation. If you passed the course, the city paid for the classes 100%...that was a blessing.

I had worked as a truck driver for the City of Phoenix for 3 ½ years; when I saw an opening for a sanitation driver. I applied and was hired for the position, under the protest of the other workers who were white and Mexican. I held the job down for about three years and finally they gave me a little break.

I was promoted to straw boss—a straw boss for my supervisor. In my new position, all I did was relay what the supervisor told me to tell the others—that's what the straw boss was for. But, unfortunately they didn't have a different pay status for that position.

I made friends with most of the people without being a "yes" man or changing my views on what I thought was right and treated everyone the same regardless of their color or nationality.

I stayed in that position for 2 ½ years, always seeking an opportunity to advance myself. I took a test to become a street inspector for the Sanitation department.

I got the job and became the first black chief inspector of Streets & Sanitation for the City of Phoenix. My job responsibilities consisted of taking complaints and information. When some of the complaints were made to the City of Phoenix, I would go to the residents to respond to their problems. As soon as they saw me, a colored man, many of them would resent me. Some would let me in, and some wouldn't. That was in the 60's.

I worked hard, steadily and consistently, and finally got promoted to the position as foreman with the City of Phoenix Streets and Sanitation Department. In keeping up with my groundbreaking track record, I had become the first black chief inspector of Streets & Sanitation.

It wasn't an easy job to be a foreman over whites and Mexicans when they resented you for being black and being their boss; but eventually they overcame the resentment and accepted the fact that changes were being made.

Chapter 28
The Analyst In Me

There was a reason why I took a few courses for management analyst and inspector of streets and sanitation—I took the exam in inspections and passed the test. Now I was in position to become the City of Phoenix' first black analyst and accepted the position when it opened up.

The inspector of streets and sanitation was responsible for answering complaints from the public, also checking alleys, streets and different conditions that were accepted by the law and the city regulations.

In my new position, it was my job to consider and analyze all these conditions. I worked approximately three years at that position; then I took an exam to be a chief inspector, passed and was promoted again. I had eight inspectors that I was responsible for. My responsibilities included: making decisions and carrying out orders that had been handed down from the higher ups on the job.

I served in that position for four years, and then took another exam to become analyst for different departments of the City of Phoenix. I passed the test and accepted the position; it was historic. I was hired as the first Black Management Analyst for the City of Phoenix, and that's the position I retired from.

Working as Management Analyst was quite a challenge, because there were so many different areas to be analyzed. For instance, there was the airport department, parks and recreation department, fire department, streets & sanitation department, garbage and trash department, transit department—those were the major departments.

The first department I was assigned to was located at the Sky Harbor International Airport. I had to start from scratch at the airport in methods improvement, to determine how much equipment, money and supplies were needed in order to get the job done. My job was to analyze the situations and make methods improvements—to help the personnel department work smarter and not harder.

The airport turned out to be a difficult area for me to analyze because the airport director out there was very prejudiced; he wasn't too pleased about me being hired out there and it was rumored that he had said there would be no "colored" people in his office while he was director. But I changed that theory—I had an office within his office. But, I managed to get by that obstacle and complete my assignment. As fate would have it, he took his vacation and after his vacation was up, he took an extended vacation and never came back to our office.

During my tenure as an analyst, I worked for the fire department, the police department and on several different hiring boards for the city of Phoenix setting up methods in improvement and implementing them.

The biggest obstacle to overcome was to change some areas in the fire department to accommodate women. Women weren't in the system because they didn't have women working there at that time. It wasn't easy; several changes had to be made, including setting up separate sleeping facilities with coed showers and restrooms.

So that women could be included in the descriptions, I also initiated changing the name firemen to fire fighters and, under my jurisdiction, policemen were renamed police officers.

Part Four

Can I

Can I hold on in this day and time
Can I be strong, can victory be mine
Can I be thorough in the work that I do
Can I be calm and be courteous too
Can I be wise in the choices I make
Can I not pass judgment in things I partake
Can I be just, can I be fair
Can I be knowledgeable, can I care
Can I speak freely about the way that I feel
Can I pray for forgiveness, can I do God's will
Can I be selective about the things in my life
Can I survive my toil and strife
Can I dream, can I be free
Can I be acknowledged for just being me?

—Yvonne Broadus

Chapter 29
I Began To See the Light

I spent a great deal of time on different projects at the international airport for the city of Phoenix.

While I worked at the airport, I got acquainted with several pilots—and learned a lot by associating with them business-wise. Lincoln Ragsdale had his own private plane in a hangar out there. He played a big part in my experiences at the airport.

Mr. Ragsdale was a successful Phoenix businessman, civil rights leader and a Tuskegee Airman—one of the first Black combat pilots in World War II. He had been on the board of directors out at the airport and would invite me to sit in on some of the meetings—for a reason. I would imagine that it was because he was the only "colored" person out there. Before I had the honor of meeting him, Mr. Ragsdale had gained much notoriety when he worked on the General Phoenix Council for Civic Unity, whose lawsuit forced desegregation of Arizona high schools in 1953, a year before the U.S. Supreme Court's landmark Brown vs. Board of Education decision.

In 1972 when I completed my airport assignment and I was recognized by the board with a certificate of outstanding commendations, issued by the new International Airport of Sky Harbor and signed by Mayor John Driggs.

A decade later, Arizona would become the last state in the Union to recognize Dr. Martin Luther King's Birthday as a Holiday. On May 9, 1986 Pastor Stewart of First Institutional Baptist Church and Senator Cloves Campbell had been instrumental in coordinating a peaceful march, which concluded at the church. After the March, there was a memorial service for

Reverend King and Governor Bruce Babbitt spoke to the people who had congregated at the First Institutional Baptist Church, declaring Reverend Martin Luther King's birthday. From that day forward, Arizona would be celebrating the third Monday of each January as a state holiday. The Governor had defied the AZ legislation; and approved the bill, which had been defeated by one vote. I took my family to the church to witness this momentous event and to be part of history in the making. We had a huge turnout the day the Governor of Arizona declared King's Birthday a legal holiday; we were so proud to participate.

Chapter 30
Making Ends Meet

I met a lot of celebrities while I worked for the city of Phoenix as an inspector for streets and sanitation and as an analyst for the firefighters, at the airport and for the police department. These contacts led to part-time situations that helped me earn extra income to make ends meet for my growing family.

The Vietnam War was on and the city was experiencing a number of financial cutbacks. For instance, refrigeration and other amenities were becoming more limited; and gas was becoming less plentiful—in fact it was rationed. As a result, many police cars in Phoenix were pulled off commission in order to save gas, which gave me an opportunity to work part-time with the Phoenix Police Department, doing time studies. So, to make ends meet, I worked for the police department and got paid for "getting ready" time, "travel" time, "reporting" time and doing "paper work" time.

During that same time period, I also entered an exciting new arena, where I met a lot of people many whom, I can still call my friends today. On my days off and at night after my day job, I worked as maitre de at Bud Brown's Barn, setting up banquets and arranging and supervising parties for some of the country's wealthiest celebrities. I covered the entire city of Phoenix—from East to West North to South—within and beyond the city limits.

I liked to cook special dishes; my favorites are beef Wellington, rack of lamb and smothered chicken with mushroom sauce. When word spread about my talent, I was asked to fix special dinners for Dr. & Mrs. Royal Davis, who was rated one of the top surgeons in the country. (Mrs. Davis is Nancy Reagan's mother and President Ronald Reagan's mother-in-law).

The Davis' lived in Chicago in the summer and in the Biltmore Estates during the winter. Dr. Davis passed away before Ms. Davis did and she would call on me to do errands and odd and ends on Saturdays while she was in Phoenix. They were beautiful people and I enjoyed being around them because they always respected me. I always looked forward to seeing them and welcoming them back to Phoenix during the winter months.

While associated with the Davis' I was also privileged to meet Sandra De O'Connor, Barry Goldwater and his family, President Richard Nixon, John Wayne, Governor Fanning, President Reagan, Governor Symington, Zsa Zsa Gabor, Merv Griffin, Frank Lloyd Wright, John and Mary Del Prizloff, the Ullmans, the Herbergers and many other prominent people in the valley. My reputation began to spread, and a demand for my cooking and catering services grew among the who's who of Phoenix.

In 1976 I met Jesse Owens at a benefit in Phoenix; he seemed to be a real calm and cool; everyone was eager to meet him and hear him speak. He proved to be an extraordinary person. Just to hear him speak and see him in person, placed him in a category all his own. At the 1936 Olympics in Berlin, Germany, Hitler was in power and his racist philosophies were prevalent. However, despite the tension, Owens won gold medals in the 100 and 200-meter sprint, the 400-meter relay, and the broad jump, setting a new world record of 25 feet, 10¼ inches.

Upon his return to the United States, Owens was disappointed with the continuing discrimination experienced by blacks. To make matters worse, he had trouble finding work. He decided to turn professional, engaging in races against a horse, a car, and other nonhuman opponents. I remember when people asked Owens about a particular race he had with a horse and he said that it was a bit exaggerated. Professional racing failed to materialize financially.

In the 1940s, Owens pursued work on the lecture circuit, which proved to be more lucrative. When I had the honor of meeting him, he had become a philanthropist and was living in the Paradise Valley area—it was a high class, expensive area to live in. Just Northwest of Scottsdale, Arizona, the small and intimate town had just been incorporated a decade earlier, in May of 1961.

The town of Paradise Valley is so beautiful, serene and surrounded by mountains; it encompasses an area of just 16.5 square miles. There are only about 5,000 homes in Paradise Valley, which is exclusively zoned for single-family residences with the cost of the average home at around $700,000. Today, the population is only around 14,000 people, with 75% of them over 18 years of age. In the sixties, many of the celebrities that I was catering for lived in Paradise Valley; it was brand new and there was so much going on out there at that time.

Civil Rights leader Lincoln Ragsdale and Jesse Owens were two of a handful African-Americans to live in Paradise Valley during the 70's. The Jesse Owens Memorial Medical Center and the Jesse Owens Memorial Track Club were established in his name and with his financial support; there is also a street named after him in South Phoenix. Jesse Owens died on March 31, 1980 in a Phoenix hospital.

Chapter 31
Divine Intervention

One of the first jobs I had when I moved to Arizona was driving a water truck for the Maricopa County Highway Department. Not being well versed on the perils of the desert, I guess you might say that I was very vulnerable.

On a typical hot summer day, one of my co-workers and I were driving in the same area; and we decided to park our trucks and stop for lunch. We both sat down under a large cottonwood tree, and as chance would have it, I encountered a rattlesnake.

There were lots of leaves on the ground and I felt something moving underneath me. I moved, and at the same time a snake tail with 18 rattles flashed out beside me, right near my head. I was shocked and, by instinct, rolled over to get out of the way. The rattlesnake bit me on the left side of my hip, thank God, where I had my wallet. It bit me so hard that it left its fang in my wallet—*I do believe that divine intervention saved my life that day.*

My fellow worker heard the snake rattling between where he was sitting and where I was sitting. He thought the snake had bitten me and insisted on taking me to the doctor; but, surprisingly, I showed him that the bite did not penetrate my skin. He killed the snake and I brought it home to show my wife Hazel and my neighbors. I kept the snake rattlers for a long time, as a conversation piece.

It had been a narrow escape. I thanked God for being on the job with me.

I have had quite a few narrow escapes, but this particular occurrence turned out to be one of the most frightening and painful experiences of my life.

It all began one day when I was climbing out of my truck at work. I stepped on a rock, twisted my ankle, and tore a ligament in my left knee. Since that occurrence, over thirty years ago, I have had five operations, including three total knee replacements on the same knee.

During my first knee replacement, while I was still in the hospital, an infection had set in and triggered a life threatening chain reaction. When I was being operated on, I developed a knee infection that spread over my entire body, which resulted in my losing all my skin, from head to toe. The infection was so bad that they feared gangrene. I had to sign for a leg amputation in case it had gone that far. I had to have a series of blood transfusions, which helped to clean out my system.

Once again, I felt I was on death's door and relied on my faith, the prayers of others and the power of God—there didn't seem to be any other way to walk out of that hospital.

Finally, after two weeks of medical attention, a series of blood transfusions and a combination of medications, the infection cleared up. So, I left the hospital and, once again, had escaped a near tragedy.

In the meantime, my doctor checked with Johnson and Johnson, the maker of the metal parts that had been inserted into my knee, and discovered that they were defective. I was in the process of suing them, but my doctor somehow *misplaced the evidence.* The case was dismissed and settled out of court.

Because of the prior unsuccessful surgery, the second total knee replacement was done almost immediately. It's no joke to have a total knee replacement; it's extremely painful and limits the movements of your body. Besides the constant pain, there's no bowling, no hunting, no walking at length—I had to give up so many of my favorite things. Three times a week, I had to see a physical therapist and because of the way I had to walk, it threw my hip out and caused back problems. So, at the age of fifty-six, because of my knee injury, I was forced into early retirement.

My knee will always give me problems, but by the grace of God, I walked out of the hospital. Although I have limitations, I just have to live with it and be careful about the way I step and walk....and I continue to count my blessings.

Chapter 32

My Eye Was On the Prize

I have a very competitive spirit; I love a challenge and I love to win; and when I do win, I love to share my moment and my rewards with those in my presence. What a great feeling!

In 1974 I had just returned from a fantastic trip to Acapulco and was feeling rather adventurous.

The California dealerships had started designing these new Chevy vans a year prior, but the car dealerships in Phoenix weren't stocking them yet. So, I decided to go to California to buy one; and I had it painted with a special design on the outside. The interior was also custom-designed, with carpeted seats and it was specially wired with surround sound—complete with a television, a stereo and music boxes. I loved the outdoors and this would be my perfect vehicle.

I was among the first in Phoenix to have an exclusive van; it was one of a kind and unique in Phoenix. So, I capitalized on it and entered a van contest. It was held at the Christown shopping center—most of the stores participated in the event and donated articles, money and gifts to the winners as an advertisement for their stores. I won first place for the *1974 Most Conservative Van of the Year* and received a plaque, some clothes, shoes and gifts from the stores that sponsored the event.

Having had so many health issues since my childhood, when I heard all the news about fitness clubs, I joined the Jack LaLane International Spa. That was 1970, and I am still a charter member there.

Shortly after I joined, I signed up thirty-five new members and received numerous gifts. For my efforts I received a special honor and award in 1973 from Mr. Jack LaLane and won a free trip for two to Acapulco for ten days. I was so happy to be able to take my wife to such a beautiful place where she and I could spend time and relax together.

The trip turned out to be one of the most memorable vacations of my life. While I was there, I went on a fishing trip and caught a ten foot, two inch sail fish weighing 138 pounds—a record fish for that part of Acapulco. Much to my delight, they had a large reception committee waiting for us on shore—and that was just the beginning. That night the Holiday Inn sponsored a huge party in my honor—I estimated 300-400 people—with food and drinks for everyone. Hazel and I really enjoyed ourselves.

Of course, I had the fish mounted and shipped to my home in Phoenix. It hangs in my office for all my friends to see and it still remains a delightful conversational piece. I also enjoy showing pictures of the sailfish as it was being caught and the struggle it put up flying through the air after it was hooked. It took one hour and fifteen exhausting and exhilarating minutes to land the powerful fish— quite an accomplishment for a man who nearly twenty-five years prior was told,

"You may only have one year to live".

Chapter 33
Living Life to the Fullest

I had always liked to go fishing and after moving to Arizona, I was fortunate enough to get around to some of the beautiful lakes in the area. As I progressed—both financially and physically—I bought and enjoyed a pontoon boat for fishing and fun with the family. (I had purchased a vacant lot next to my home and kept the boat there). It had 125 horsepower motor and was covered and enclosed. The boat was large enough to carry twelve or fifteen people, and we always had a great mix—those who wanted to fish, or those who just wanted to ride for pleasure.

That was such fun; our family and friends would go on picnics and enjoy the water so much, especially when it was hot in Phoenix. I took lessons on boating laws and was involved in boating safety.

Hazel and I also took swimming lessons, just in case we needed to swim for our own safety and assist those who may need my help. It was so convenient, because the swimming instructor came right to our pool to teach us. The lessons came in handy because my grandchildren were always in the water. We had the only large pool in the area and, at times, it was so full that it seemed like a community pool. We really enjoyed people and invited many of the neighborhood children and their families to visit.

Sometimes, I would go hunting for big game. On one of my hunting trips, I managed to get a four-prong white tail deer. I had the deer's head mounted and put it in my office with the other trophies—a mallet duck and some special fish.

I even took up dancing lessons with Arthur Murray Studios for exercise and to distinguish with more accuracy the movements from my left foot to my right foot. I learned the tango and the waltz and got a certificate for completing the classes. This turned out to be one of the most enjoyable activities I shared with my wife Hazel.

Not too long ago, Hazel and I managed to take a seven-day cruise to Hawaii where we visited the five islands. It was very exciting; we went with three other couples. It was our first trip abroad and we enjoyed every day of the trip; especially the day we went to visit the USS Arizona ship. That experience was very interesting, to see where the Japanese battled with us and grasp a better understanding of why we had to use the atomic weapon.

Much of my recreation and pleasure comes from time spent with my friends and family. Hazel and I never miss a holiday or birthday with our children and grandchildren; I believe that the comradeship of a close-knit and loving family is one of the greatest gifts a man can have.

Chapter 34
The Strickland Family

My Father James Monroe Strickland was born in North Carolina in 1867. He had a stroke in 1945 and died on Long Island, New York in 1953 at the age of 86.

My Mother Sarah Jane (Smith) Strickland died of cancer in 1963. After my father died, I drove back to New York with my family and convinced my mother to come out to Arizona (because she did have a little arthritis) and I thought the hot weather in Arizona would serve her well the rest of her days. She came back with us and stayed for a few months, but got homesick—she just had to go back to New York.

My mother had never flown on a plane before, but she was willing to fly back this time. I always believed she wanted to go back to New York because my father was buried there. She went back; and within a year or so, she passed away and was buried next to my father on Long island. Sarah Jane (Smith) Strickland was a devoted mother and wife, a very religious woman and a true believer in God's love.

My seven half brothers and sisters, Cyrus "Roscoe", Cora, Donie, Dothulle, Leanna, James and Sanford "Robert", were all born to Gertrude Penn Strickland and James Strickland in Virginia. They are all deceased now. Roscoe was the youngest half-brother and closest to my age. Roscoe and my two youngest sisters Cora and Donie moved to Long Island with my mother and father; my other half brothers and sisters remained in North Carolina. Roscoe had four children: Yvonne, Cyrus, Jr., Gertrude and Gale. Roscoe's widow Helen Strickland and daughter Yvonne Strickland David live in Phoenix, Arizona with Yvonne's husband Alphonse "Jack" David. Cora Strickland Flippen had six children: Algernon, Rowena, Clara, Charles, Curtis and Vanette. Donie Strickland Travis had five children: Johnny, Nathan, James, Betsy and Della.

Four of Sarah and James' children—my other seven brothers and sisters (Beatrice, Samuel, Matthew and Louvinia) are deceased; those three surviving siblings are Herman, Viola and Arthur. Herman lives in Stuart, Virginia; Viola lives in Long Island; and Arthur lives in Phoenix.

My older sister Beatrice was the first sibling to leave home. She and her husband Willie Harvey had three girls. After living in New York for many years, Bea and Reuben came to live with us in Phoenix where she died. Bea is survived by her three daughters (Elizabeth, Beatrice and Joyce) and their children.

My brother Samuel was the second sibling to leave home. He got married but didn't have any children. Samuel had an accident on his job and had to have surgery on his back. He never did pull through; sadly he died from that accident on the job.

My other Brother Peter "Matthew" Strickland, Sr. was the third oldest of Sarah and James' children. He married and had five children (Adelaide, Peter, Carol, James and Linda). Matthew was a Preacher at the First Baptist Church of Cutchogue (Long Island), New York. After serving as Associate Minister, he received his Preacher's license in 1983. Matthew was an active member of the First Baptist Church for over thirty-nine years. He was employed at the North Fork Bank and Trust Company for nineteen years until he retired in November 1984. Matthew died a year later at the age of sixty-six.

My next brother, Herman Strickland is three years my senior. Herman got married and had one son, Herman, Jr. with his first wife Mary. At the age of sixty-nine Herman remarried; and he and his second wife Eleanor adopted an infant girl, Lisa, and later adopted her two boys. Herman's wife died a few years ago.

Sara Jane Strickland, age 65, Long Island, NY

Sam Smith, Robuster's grandfather (taken in Ararat, VA)

Buster's sister Beatrice Evans

Buster's sister Beatrice Strickland Evans and her husband, Reuben Evans (both deceased)

121

Robuster's brother, Arthur Strickland, age 19

Beatrice Strickland Harvey (Buster's sister), Long Island, NY

Louvina Strickland, Robuster's sister

Robuster's brother, Herman Strickland

Mabel and Sam Strickland, Buster's brother and his wife (taken in Long Island, NY)

Sarah Strickland (Buster's mother) taken in the yard of her home, Long Island, NY

Jack and Yvonne David, niece and husband, Riverhead, Long Island, NY

Buster's half-sister Leana Travis and her daughter, Beatrice, in Mount Airy, NC, 1991

Buster's half-sister Leana Travis and her daughter, Alice, in Mount Airy, NC

Roscoe, Robuster's half-brother, at home in Long Island, NY

Siblings: Beatrice Matthew, Louvinia, Herman, Viola, Buster in Long Island, NY

Hazel, Robuster, brother Roscoe, with Buster's nieces and nephews at Coney Island, NY

Robuster's brother, Herman; mother; and brother, Matthew, Long Island

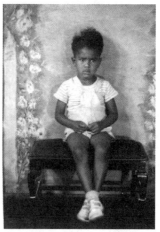

Peter Strickland, nephew, Long Island, NY

Lou Ethel, Buster's sister-in-law; Sarah Strickland, mother; and sister Cora (half-siser)

My sister Viola is two years younger than me. She got married in 1947 to Harvey Cain; the couple had three children—two boys (Reginald and Ronald) and one girl (Vanessa). (Ronald died from cancer at the age of 51.) When Viola and Harvey were divorced, she visited me in Arizona and met and married Emmet Cross, who she eventually separated from. Viola who lives in Cutchogue, Long Island ultimately pursued a career in nursing. She graduated from New York City Central School for Licensed practical Nursing in 1958 and from Liberty Bible College in Lynchburg, Virginia in 1979.

My brother Arthur Strickland is five years younger than me. He lives in Arizona with his wife Lenore. Arthur has two children (Edward and Nancy) by a previous marriage. He retired from the City of Phoenix Sanitation Department, where he was a supervisor.

My baby sister Louvinia and her husband John Ford lived on Long Island, New York and raised four children (Janie, Tommy, Kevin and Darlene). After my mother returned to New York from Phoenix, Louvinia cared for her until she died. Louvinia developed Multiple Sclerosis and died in 1999.

Chapter 35
The Roberts Family

Like my father, my wife Hazel's father Early Roberts was a sharecropper; he harvested tobacco in North Carolina. Hazel's mother Carrie Roberts helped out on the farm, but would have to go home early to prepare dinner for the family. Because of a growing family of seven children, Carrie eventually stopped farming to work at home full time.

After Early quit working on the farm, he chose to remain in the South. (Did he work in the quarry?) He worked at a laundry in Mount Airy, North Carolina where he starched the clothes by hand. When Hazel was a teenager, she worked with her dad in the laundry where she was a presser.

Early Roberts worked in the laundry until he retired. He had saved enough money to buy the family a home on four acres of land lavished by apple trees, peach trees and a huge garden with every vegetable garden imaginable. The property was also enriched by a well; Hazel was thrilled because they didn't have to go to the spring for water anymore.

Mr. Roberts was a deacon at the same church for fifty years; Mrs. Roberts was the Mother of the church for just as many years. I can truthfully say they were the finest in-laws that a person could ask for and they accepted me like I was part of their own family.

Carrie Roberts (47) and Early Roberts (48), parents of Hazel (taken in Mount Airy, NC

Carrie Sawyers Roberts, mother of Hazel Strickland, age 18 (taken in Ararat, VA in 1913)

Hazel E. Roberts, 6 months old (taken in Ararat, VA)

Hazel's grandfather

Hazel's brother, Gentry and wife Elaine

Hazel's brother, Gentry, and wife Elaine, my niece, nephew and brother- in-law, Brady in Mount Airy, NC

The Roberts Family Reunion: Mr. and Mrs. Early Roberts, children, grandchildren. Buster and Hazel were visiting from Arizona with three children,

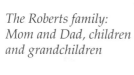

The Roberts family: Mom and Dad, children and grandchildren

Hazel's 60th high school reunion in Mount Airy, NC in 2002 with sisters and brothers and their families (Jones High School)

Hazel's sisters and brother, Gentry, Aaron, Pearl, Hazel, Frances, Clarence at church in Ararat, VA

Hazel's mother developed sugar diabetes. She lived a couple of years with one leg amputated and passed away August 1975 at 80 years old. Hazel's dad passed away five years later from a heart attack, September 2nd in 1979; he was 86 years old.

Hazel has three sisters (Frances, Pearl and Mabel) and two brothers (Gentry and Aaron). Her third and oldest brother, Clarence, passed away at the age of 68. Two of Hazel's sisters reside in New York, one sister resides in North Carolina and two brothers reside in Virginia.

Chapter 36
Sharing My Blessings

I became a charter member at the Elks Lodge where I served on the board of trustees for eight years. The Elks Lodge is a charitable non-profitable organization, which helps underprivileged families. They provide food for needy in times, especially during Thanksgiving and Christmas, as well as gifts for children. The Elks also donate scholarships to different schools and classes, in addition to being involved with other essential community causes. I received a medal of honor for 50 years service as an Elk and am still a charter member.

I have also served on the board for the Wesley Community Center, which is dedicated to helping children. This is a non-profit organization located in the areas where underprivileged children live. The Center helps keep youngsters off the streets by organizing different programs so they can become active in sports, and they work with children who have reading and writing difficulties.

For more than ten years, I have been on the Board of Directors at the Ebony House, which is an organization for men who are drug addicts. After I retired from my job, I had more time to dedicate toward community programs; I decided to involve the local farmers. I had maintained my connections with the farmers from the time I grew my own small crops in South Phoenix; and those farmers donate their excess potatoes, grapes, onions, and corn to the Ebony House.

I remember one time when a farmer donated watermelons; he told me to take as many as I could carry in my van; and, of course, I filled it up. I was driving down Baseline Road, one of the main roads in Phoenix, and my door flew open. Before I could stop the truck and close the door, watermelons were scattered all along Baseline Road. At the time, it was frightening; but when I think back, it had to be very comical.

I will continue to serve on the Board of the Ebony House as well as the newly established Elba House (for female addicts), for as long as they need me. I hope that my contribution can make a difference to those men and women in some small way.

On November 11, 2004, one week after my 81st birthday, I was honored by Blue Cross and Blue Shield of Arizona and the Arizona Republic as an Ageless Hero. Much to my surprise, I was the grand prize-winner in the category of *Vigor and Vitality* for my ability to perform agile feats, both mental and physical.

When they called my name, the announcer stated: "Buster is known as 'an active gem in the African-American community because he wants to help everyone he meets.' In addition to his community involvement, Buster is a strong family person who always initiates family activities with his wife Hazel Strickland and their three children—Marilyn, Rochelle and Kenneth and his grandchildren."

In addition to my community involvement, I have been an active member of the First Institutional Baptist Church since 1949, where Hazel and I sang in the choir. I also served on the Board of Trustees.

I must say that I take delight in everything I do and I feel that by helping others, my blessings continue to flow… and, I thank God for every breath that I take…and for every day that I wake.

In Conclusion...

I was given many opportunities to succeed by people helping me; and in return, I get enjoyment by helping others. It is my prayer that, this book will help you know me better and give you a reason to smile. We all have obstacles to overcome, but if you focus on living your life to the fullest and discover the joy of giving then your road will be a lot smoother.

I would like to leave this world a better place than I found it. Yesterday is history. Tomorrow is a mystery. Today is a gift—that's why they call it "the present".

The Lord has blessed me health-wise and in many other ways.... and I thank Him.

—Robuster Strickland

These are they who never found it too hot in the summer
or cold in the winter to trudge the old dirt roads to their church
to give praise to God for His loving kindness in sparing them to see
another Sunday
so they could glorify His holy name....
These are they who mounted up with wings as eagles,
ran and did not get weary and did not faint.
They just kept on keeping on, because they walked by faith, not by sight!

—Author Unknown,
From the memorial to Sam and Minnie Hughes

Epilogue—Recalling My Roots

Saturday May 24, 2003 a memorial garden was dedicated to the free black men and women who farmed one hundred years ago in Stokes and Surry counties. The garden is located on Athey Simmons Road and Charles McArthur Road in the Chestnut Ridge area about eight miles east of Mount Airy, North Carolina.

One of the organizers for the dedication was Nathaniel McArthur who stated, "The first black (African-American) farmers began moving to Mount Airy around 1889. They began to share the responsibility of building one-room log cabins and clearing the land for farming. Cross-cut, two man saws and axes were the main tools used to raise a cabin in one week. Red mud was used to seal up the cracks; shingles rived from chestnut trees by hand were used for roofing. They had no machinery for farming, their sole way of surviving."

Upon entering the grounds of the garden, I got a chill just remembering and visualizing all the emotions of our newly freed ancestors. Knowing the pain, suffering, struggles and determination that were required just to survive during those times set my heart racing. But, I also realized how much joy, love and kinship there must have been for those men and women (our ancestors) who had the strength to plant their roots and pass on to so many families this proud heritage.

I've already shared my father's story of how, after an altercation, he fled to Long Island with his wife and children in tow. Some of our relatives did, however, remain in the area and many of their children and grandchildren have either remained in Mount Airy or relocated there. In fact, my nephew, the Reverend James

Strickland led the prayer at the Memorial Garden Dedication Ceremony.

There are many stories to remember and to pass down through the generations...stories that exemplify the persistence of the many farmers who lived as sharecroppers, the sons and daughters of slaves, who overcame the obstacles of a small southern community and acquired land.

For instance, in 1899, George Robert McArthur II and his wife Ida purchased and moved on to a 93-acre tract of land at a cost of fifty cents per acre ($46.50). By 1910, the McArthurs were conducting weekly meetings to share their knowledge and experience, which helped them become more productive tobacco farmers. More than one hundred years later the same farmland still remains in the McArthur family.

The farming community prospered and grew. Samuel "Fletcher" Jessup and his wife Mary had ten children. He was a tireless farmer and benevolent man who evidenced a strong interest in the community. In 1906, the Jessups deeded the first of several parcels of their land to the Surry County Board of Education for the establishment of a school for colored children; in 1912, they deeded another portion of their land to the Trustees of the Chestnut Ridge Progressive Primitive Baptist Church for the construction of a church and the establishment of a church cemetery.

The depression of 1932 hit the black farmers hard. Many other black farmers purchased as much as 600 acres or as little as 25 acres for just fifty cents an acre; a few would keep their land; most would lose it....foreclosed for owing as little as $60.

The memorial garden was built on the McArthurs' land, established to honor and give tribute to those men and women who had the courage to stand up against the odds. It is the land where my father farmed; it is the land that held my parents' home; it is the land on which I entered this earth. I am grateful that the McArthurs had the vision and the willingness to share our brave ancestors' history with all who wish to visit.

In the memorial garden, granite monuments are inscribed with the names of forty-two men identified as "the Free Historical Black Farmers of Chestnut Ridge, Slate Mountain, Mount Herman and Westfield." Many of them still have families living in the area.

Those free black men, born between the years of 1842 and 1902, who led the way to the Mount Airy community:

▼ Clark—Melton Clark

▼ Copeney—George Copeney, Henry Copeney

▼ Cox—Bart Cox

▼ Dearmon—Clennon Dearmon

▼ Finney—John Finney

▼ Flippen—Tom Flippen

▼ France—Floyd France, Rufus France

▼ Gilbert—Tommy Gilbert

▼ Hatcher—Adam Hatcher, Arthur Hatcher, Henry Hatcher, Herbert Hatcher, Joe Hatcher, Sam Hatcher, Tommie Hatcher

▼ Hughes—Sam Hughes

▼ Jessup—Fletcher Jessup, Virlen Jessup

▼ McArthur—Brice McArthur, Charlie McArthur, Robert McArthur

▼ Mills—Joe Mills, Willie Mills

- ▼ Moore—Bandy Moore, Colonel Moore, Early Moore, Robert Moore, Walter Moore, Willis Moore

- ▼ Penn—Vester Penn, Zeffie Penn

- ▼ Ross—Jim Ross, Sandy Ross

- ▼ Simmons—Charlie Simmons

- ▼ Smith—Joe Smith, John Smith, Payne Smith, Pinkney Smith,

- ▼ Strickland—My father Jim Strickland and my uncle George Strickland are among those memorialized at the garden.

It is because of the multitudes of brave men…and women…like my father, mother, grandfather, grandmother, aunts, uncles …and all my ancestors who challenged the system and rose up from the many obstacles in their lives that I am here to tell my story. My success is their success and; and I hope you will feel the spirit of your ancestors like I do and pass it on to our new generations.

—Robuster Strickland

Appendix A
Certificates and Awards

I've loved my life. With all I've done, there's still more to do. I've had to change course a few times, but *I'VE NEVER LOOKED BACK.* Just knowing that my efforts have been appreciated makes me very fulfilled and blessed. Here is a review of my life through some of my certificates and awards:

1. Certificate of Promotion – June 23, 1938

2. Neighborhood Playhouse for Children Reference Letter – September 19, 1949

3. Institute for Training in Municipal Administration Certificate – March 17, 1958

4. Phoenix Evening College Commendation – May 21, 1962

5. City of Phoenix, Arizona Certificate of In-Service Training – February 1, 1967

6. Phoenix Sky Harbor Airport Certificate of Commendation – January 17, 1972

7. First Institutional Baptist Church 30 Years of Service Certificate of Honor – August 28, 1983

8. US Coast Guard Auxiliary Boating Skills and Seamanship Certificate – November 28, 1983

9. Howard Harrison Athletic Award for Swimming – December, 1983

10. AZ Game & Fish Department Boating Safety Certificate – December 14, 1983

11. Arthur Murray Dance Schools Certificate of merit – May 4, 1986

12. Elks Lodge Certificate for 50 Years of Service and Dedication – August 13, 2000

13. Office of the Governor (Fife Symington) of AZ Special Recognition – September 3, 1994

14. First Institutional Baptist Church Longevity Award – September 3, 2004

15. Blue Cross Blue Shield & AZ Republic Ageless Hero Award – November 11, 2004

Certificate of Promotion

This Certifies that

Robuster, Strickland

Has successfully completed the course of study prescribed for the _7th_ Grade, and is therefore entitled to this Testimonial and Admission to the _8th_ Grade.

Given at _Oregon School_ this _twenty-third_ Day of _June_ 19_38_

Emily Falkowski.

THE
Neighborhood Playhouse for Children

1865 East 8th Street • Brooklyn 23, N. Y.

ESplanade 5-2155

HAROLD LEWIS, Director

September 19, 1949

To Whom It May Concern:

Mr. Robuster Strickland, of 754 Cauldwell Avenue, Bronx, New York, was employed by us as Chauffeur and General Maintenance Man from December 20, 1944 through August 31, 1949.

During all of that near-five year period he proved to be exceptionally well suited to his job; an excellent and careful driver, handy with all types of tools, personable, friendly, cooperative, intelligent, and completely trustworthy.

We consider Buster's leaving a real loss to us and would unqualifiedly recommend him for any job that it is felt he can handle.

Respectfully yours,

Harold Lewis, Adm. Dir.

The Neighborhood Playhouse for Children

REGISTERED. UNIVERSITY OF THE STATE OF NEW YORK.
STATE DEPARTMENT OF EDUCATION ALBANY, N. Y.

INSTITUTE FOR TRAINING IN MUNICIPAL ADMINISTRATION

Conducted by

THE INTERNATIONAL CITY MANAGERS' ASSOCIATION

CHICAGO

THIS CERTIFICATE

IS AWARDED TO

Robuster Strickland

WHO HAS SATISFACTORILY COMPLETED AN EXTENSION COURSE IN

Local Planning Administration

March 17, 1958

Director

Instructor

Phoenix Evening College

Commends

ROBUSTER STRICKLAND

for satisfactorily completing

SUPERVISORY PERSONNEL DEVELOPMENT

Instructor

May 21, ___ 19 62

Dean

146

CITY OF PHOENIX, ARIZONA
PERSONNEL DEPARTMENT

CERTIFICATE OF IN-SERVICE TRAINING

This is to certify that

ROBUSTER STRICKLAND

has satisfactorily completed the following course

EFFECTIVE SUPERVISORY PRACTICES

Awarded this _____First_____ *day of* February, 1967

_____
City Manager

_____
Personnel Director

PHOENIX SKY HARBOR
International Airport

Presents this Certificate of Commendation to **Robuster Strickland** for participating in ceremonies dedicating a new International Arrivals Building and officially making Phoenix Sky Harbor International Airport an International Port of Entry.

Conferred on January 17, 1972

_____
Mayor of the City of Phoenix

147

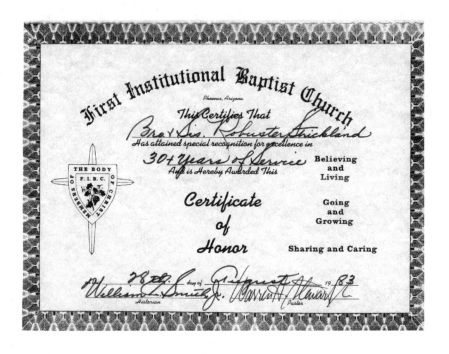

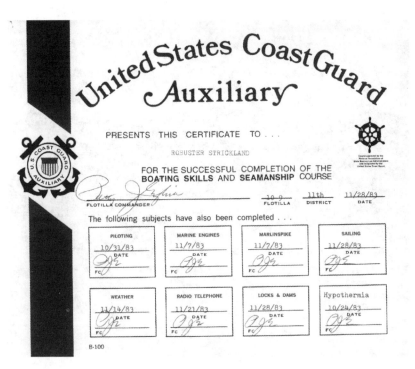

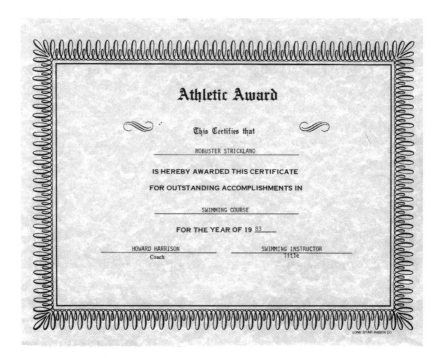

Athletic Award

This Certifies that

ROBUSTER STRICKLAND

IS HEREBY AWARDED THIS CERTIFICATE

FOR OUTSTANDING ACCOMPLISHMENTS IN

SWIMMING COURSE

FOR THE YEAR OF 19 83

HOWARD HARRISON	SWIMMING INSTRUCTOR
Coach	Title

LONE STAR RIBBON CO.

STATE OF ARIZONA
ARIZONA GAME AND FISH DEPARTMENT

AWARDS THIS CERTIFICATE TO

ROBUSTER STRICKLAND

**FOR SATISFACTORY COMPLETION OF A COURSE IN
ARIZONA BOATING SAFETY TRAINING**

PRESENTED THIS 14th **DAY OF** December 19 83

State Boating Administrator

Director, Game and Fish Department

149

𝕬rthur 𝕸urray® 𝕯ance 𝕾chools
𝕾ocial and 𝕮ompetition 𝕾tandards of 𝕭allroom 𝕯ancing

AMATEUR DANCING
CERTIFICATE of MERIT

𝕭ronze I
social 𝕾tandard

awarded to

𝕭uster 𝕾trickland

IN RECOGNITION OF THE COMPLETION AND FULFILLMENT OF
THE REQUIREMENTS OF THE ABOVE STANDARD OF BALLROOM DANCING.

𝕬rthur 𝕸urray 𝕯ance 𝕾chool

OF _Phoenix City_ A FRANCHISED SCHOOL

BY _J. R. DuBois_ FRANCHISEE

Mark Peck STUDIO OR CERTIFIED EXAMINER

_5/4/86_ DATE

Smooth

CERTIFICATE
FOR

SPECIAL RECOGNITION

This Certifies That

Robuster Strickland

is awarded this Certificate for

_____50+ years of service and dedication_____

Given at _Wm. H. Patterson Lodge #477_, this _13th_ day of _August_, 2000

Michael E. Johnson
EXALTED RULER

Ananias Mason
SECRETARY

Fife Symington
Governor

Office of the Governor

WITH SPECIAL RECOGNITION

to

Hazel and Buster Strickland

September 3, 1994
50th Wedding Anniversary

*A lasting marriage, the cornerstone of a family,
is the most important product our state can produce.*

Your 50 years together is a tribute to you both and to Arizona.

May God bless you as you continue your life together.

IN WITNESS WHEREOF, I have hereunto
set my hand and caused to be affixed the
Great Seal of the State of Arizona, done at
the Capitol in Phoenix on this
first day of September in the year
of our Lord One Thousand Nine
Hundred and Ninety-four.

GOVERNOR

F.I.B.C. MARRIAGE MINISTRY LONGEVITY AWARD

PRESENTED **SEPTEMBER 3, 2004** TO

ROBUSTER & HAZEL

STRICKLAND

In recognition for your faithful service to
one another for 60 years of marriage

"Serving our Spouses by Acknowledging their Needs and Desires"
Galatians 5:13; Ephesians 5:22-23; Mark 10:6-9

First Institutional Baptist Church
The Reverends Tommy and Nancy Reynolds, Ministry Co-Chairs
Dr. Warren H. Stewart, Sr., Senior Pastor

THE ARIZONA REPUBLIC

MONDAY, NOVEMBER 22, 2004   azcentral.com   50 CENTS

AHWATUKEE

Busy giver is 1 of 'Ageless Heroes'

By Lars Jacoby
lars.jacoby@arizonarepublic.com

Robuster "Buster" Strickland has been living on borrowed time since 1949.

Before coming to Arizona, doctors gave him a year to live because of his severe asthma and chronic pneumonia. Once Strickland arrived in Arizona, he knew he was going to be fine.

"As soon as I stepped off the plane I could breathe, I knew right then," said Strickland, 81, of Ahwatukee Foothills.

After several jobs, Strickland was hired by Phoenix and worked his way up the ladder.

"Being a Black man, I always had to prove myself," said Strickland, who started as a garbage truck driver and retired from a management position in 1979. Since then, he has made giving back a priority.

"I've been quite busy," said Strickland, the recipient of the 2004 Ageless Heroes award, sponsored by Blue Cross Blue Shield of Arizona and The Arizona Republic.

The annual awards recognize residents 65 and older who serve as "a role model for living life to the fullest." He was honored for volunteering with the Wesley Community Center, the Elk's Lodge, First Institutional Baptist Church and Ebony House, a drug rehabilitation facility.

Mike Ryosarzon/The Arizona Republic
Robuster Strickland and his wife, Hazel, of 60 years, pose in the living room of their Phoenix home, with Robuster's award given to him for his volunteer work, by Blue Cross and Blue Shield.

Southeast Valley Ageless Heroes finalists

Champion for Health:
■ Betty Byrne, 82, of Mesa. Byrne has been a volunteer at Banner Hospital for more than 20 years. Currently, she is a trainer in the pet therapy program, which visits patients and families at the hospital.
■ Dr. Leland Fairbanks, 73, of Tempe. Fairbanks has been working to ban secondhand tobacco smoke from indoor places since 1957. In 1983, his efforts led the Hopi Hospital in Keams Canyon to become the nation's first smoke-free hospital. He currently works with Smokefree Arizona to further the cause.

Love of Learning:
■ Martha Watkins, 80, of Gold Canyon. In her 50s, Watkins returned to college to become an English teacher. Watkins still substitute teaches two to three days a week at Apache Junction High School. She also teaches basic English to Spanish-speaking construction workers.

Appendix B
I Can Cook! Buster's Best Recipes

I have a good sense of taste that fits the taste buds of most people and I feel real comfortable in the kitchen trying different recipes. This book wouldn't be complete without sharing some of my favorite recipes with you. Enjoy!

Buster's Chicken & Sausage or Seafood Gumbo

2 tablespoons of olive oil
2 ½ cups diced carrots
2 ½ cups diced celery
1 ½ cups diced yellow onions
1 tablespoon minced garlic
1 ½ cups of diced carrots
1 large can diced tomatoes
½ cup tomato sauce
2 teaspoons full of vegetable base
8 ounces okra
6 cups water
1 ½ tablespoons of Cajun seasoning
salt & pepper to taste
¼ to ½ cup of gumbo filet*
6-8 oz of cooked chicken cubes
1 pound of peeled shrimp (or other shellfish)
or, if you prefer, substitute the seafood with sausage (6 cooked sausages)

Shrimp should be peeled and put in to brown in a heavy bottom stock pot.

Heat the olive oil over medium high heat.

All meat that is used should be cooked in the olive oil.

Add the carrots, celery onions and garlic and sauté' until softened (about 5 minutes)

Add diced tomatoes, tomato sauce and vegetables; cook for 5 minutes, stirring often.

Mix in okra and water and bring to a boil; reduce heat and simmer 10 minutes.

Add Cajun seasoning and salt and pepper to taste.

Carefully sprinkle in gumbo filet, stirring gently to prevent the filet from lumping up.

Add cooked chicken and shrimp, and/or sausage (as you like); heat 5 minutes more; then serve

Makes 6 to 8 servings

Note: *Gumbo filet is a thickener made from brown dried sassafras leaves. Look for it in the spice section or specialty food section of your grocery store

This recipe came from my older brother Sam. When I was a teenager in Long Island, I would go to his house and hang out with him. He also enjoyed cooking and one day prepared this very tasty dish, which I just had to have every time I visited him. Sam taught me how to make Gumbo and through the years I added a few little extras. My favorite is Seafood Gumbo with the works...crabs, oysters, shrimp and lobster. Enjoy!!!

Buster's Chili Con Queso

1 3 lb block of Velveeta cheese
1 large can of whole tomatoes
1 tall can of roasted chiles

Dice the cheese and put it in the top of a double boiler.

Cook and stir the cheese until it begins to melt.

Strain the tomatoes and use only the pulp.

Add the tomatoes to the Velveeta cheese in the double boiler.

Cook the cheese and tomatoes slowly, stirring constantly.

Remove seeds from the chiles and cut them up real fine

Stir the chiles into the cheese mixture.

Make 8 to 10 servings

Serve **Buster's Chili Con Queso** warm with tortilla chips.

I hope you have enjoyed my recipe. Now you know how quick and easy it is to make my chili con queso. Put it together whenever you have guests and I guarantee that they will sing you many praises.

Buster's Original Potato Soup

1 pound of sliced bacon
1 cup of margarine
1 cup of all-purpose flour
8 cups of milk
5 large potatoes chipped in small pieces and cubed (cooked)
2-4 green onions, chopped
1 ¼ cup shredded cheddar cheese
1 ½ cup sour cream
1 teaspoon salt or season to taste
1 ½ teaspoon ground black pepper

Place bacon in a large deep skillet; cook over medium heat until brown/crisp. Drain and crumble the bacon and set it aside

Cook the potatoes in a stock pot or Dutch oven

In a separate pot, melt the margarine over medium heat; whisk in the flour until smooth; and gradually stir in the milk, whisking constantly until thickened

Stir in the potatoes and onions (onions should be cut up real fine)

Bring to a boil, stirring frequently; then reduce heat and simmer 10 minutes

Mix in salt, pepper, bacon, cheese and sour cream and continue cooking, stirring frequently until cheese is melted.

Makes 8 servings

We were raised on a potato farm on Long Island, so quite naturally, potatoes were always plentiful in our home. My mother cooked potatoes for us almost every day. She originated all kinds of recipes from potatoes; and I still enjoy cooking and eating them every chance I get. There's baked potatoes, French fries, au gratin potatoes, scalloped potatoes, mashed potatoes, hash brown potatoes, potato pancakes and many more....and of course, there's my favorite...Buster's Original Potato Soup. Try it! I guarantee you'll like it!

Busters Original Broccoli Salad

1 large bunch of broccoli
1 medium onion
2 medium shredded carrots
1 lb bacon cooked crisp
1 ½ cups raisins
2 ½ - 3 tablespoons vinegar
1 ½ cups salad dressing**
½ cup sugar

Chop broccoli, onions and carrots into small pieces

Combine broccoli, onion, carrots, bacon and raisins in a large bowl.

In a separate bow, combine Miracle Whip and poppy seed dressing in equal proportions.

Add sugar and vinegar to the salad dressing.

At the last minute, just before you serve the salad, pour the dressing mix over the vegetables and toss thoroughly.

Makes 6 servings

This delectable salad is a result of my experimenting one day. I didn't have any lettuce in the house, but I felt like having a salad. So, I used what I had on hand and came up with one of my most popular dishes, and best of all....it's very healthy.

Buster's Old Fashioned Deep Dish Apple Pie

1 Pillsbury frozen deep-dish piecrust
½ cup brown sugar
¾ cups granulated sugar
½ cup all purpose flour
1 small packet of spice
½ cup butter or margarine
6 cups of peeled and thinly sliced apples
½ cup quick cooking oats

Heat oven to 4oo degrees, place cookie sheet on oven rack.

In large bowl, stir together granulated sugar, spice packet and apples.

Spoon mixture into frozen crust.

In medium bowl, stir together brown sugar, flour and butter until it is crumbly; then stir in oats.

Sprinkle mixture over the filling.

Bake pie on cookie sheet 40 to 50 minutes or until filling is bubbly.

Serves 8 people.

While I was growing up, fruit was always plentiful, especially apples. Of course, my mother made some of the best apple dishes around. There were many occasions when I couldn't play outside because of my asthma, so I spent a lot of quality time in the kitchen with my mother. For those of you, who have a sweet tooth, I thought I'd share one of my favorite desserts…straight from my mother's kitchen.

Buster's Red Velvet Cake

1-teaspoon vanilla
1 teaspoons salt
½ cup solid shortening
1 ½ cups sugar
2 eggs
1 teaspoon vanilla
2 tablespoons cocoa
2 ½ ounces red food coloring
1 cup buttermilk
2 cups all purpose flour
1 ½ teaspoons baking soda
1 ½ tablespoons vinegar

Heat oven to about 350

Grease and flour a 9 X 13 inch pan.

In a large mixing bowl, cream together the sugar, salt and the shortening.

Add eggs and vanilla, and mix well.

In a small bowl, dissolve cocoa and food coloring; and stir well.

Pour over cream mixture and mix well.

Add buttermilk and flour to the mixture, alternately mixing after each addition.

In a cup, mix baking soda and vinegar and blend into the batter.

Bake for about 30 minutes or test cake test; it is done when a toothpick inserted near the center of the cake comes out dry.

Cool cake about 10 minutes before removing it from pan(s).

You can either make the frosting or you can buy the ready mixed. Here's how I do it:

Buster's Best Frosting

1 package of softened cream cheese (3 ounces)
1 pound package of powdered sugar
¼ teaspoon vanilla
½ cup softened margarine

In a large mixing bowl, combine cream cheese, margarine, powdered sugar and vanilla.

Mix until smooth (use electric mixer to blend better)

Spread frosting over cooled cake.

Makes 12-15 servings.

As a child, I never experienced Red Velvet Cake; it was brought to my attention much later, while I was living in Arizona. A friend of ours, Ms. Moore, used to give my family a homemade cake every year for Christmas. Believe me, it was mouthwatering; and I pestered her until she gave me the recipe. Because I love to experiment in the kitchen, I added a few new ingredients, and came up with Buster's Red Velvet Cake. Thank you Ms. Moore!

Appendix C
More Praise for Robuster Strickland

I am Buster Strickland's younger brother by 5 years. When he was growing up, my brother Buster had a very severe case of asthma.

He had taken a job with a local bakery and there were times his asthma would get so bad that I would get up very early in the morning to help him load the bakery products in Riverhead, New York. Then we would deliver them to an outlet in Greenport, New York about 15 miles away.

When Buster's asthma would become severe, the only way he could sleep was in a crouched position on his knees, on his bed. Buster's asthma became so bad that the doctor treating him suggested he move to Arizona because, as he stated "It may be your only chance to live." After Buster arrived in Arizona his asthma, amazingly, began to improve.

I really admired Buster for being able to overcome his medical condition. He could have given up so easily, but he didn't. Instead he demonstrated courage and strength, and went on to lead a very productive life.

—Arthur E. Strickland, Buster's brother

My brother-in-law Buster was always one of my favorite people. I hadn't seen Buster in almost twenty years when I went to Phoenix for my son's wedding in the 1970's; but he and Hazel welcomed me into their home with open arms. They took me sightseeing, out to dinner and really spoiled me. After my husband Roscoe Strickland died, I moved from Long, Island (New York) to Phoenix, where I live with my daughter Yvonne. Whenever I see Buster, I know it's going to be a wonderful experience; he always makes you feel like royalty.

—Helen Strickland, Sister-in-Law

I have known Uncle Buster since I was a little girl, and my husband Jack David has known him for the past 23 years.

Uncle Buster is one of the nicest, most hard-working, busiest human beings you'll ever meet. His other attributes are that he is extremely kindhearted, caring, concerned, generous, fun loving, and one who never meets a stranger. He treats everyone he meets with the highest dignity and respect. Uncle Buster, truly, is his brother's keeper, just as Jesus has asked each of us to be.

In addition he has been a wonderful uncle to me and to our family, and a great friend/father figure to Jack. We, and our entire family love him dearly. It is clearly evident by the friends and acquaintances he's made over the years that he knows just about everyone in the Phoenix area. That's why I asked him years ago why he didn't run for a political office? I told him that he would have won by a landslide!!!

—Yvonne Strickland David, Executive Sales Associate, Coldwell Banker Success Realty and Alphonse (Jack) David, retired US Air Force (Buster's niece and nephew-in-law)

Buster, I would like to begin with a sincere "Thank you!".

Thank you for being such an inspiration to the Roberts Family since marrying my sister. Thanks for being the husband that you are, the father that you are and the special brother-in-law that you have been to me. Thank you, Buster, for keeping our family close, even though we are many miles apart.

This book will be a written testimony of your life as well as a remarkable accomplishment. The Bible states, "In Him, we have boldness and access with confidence through faith...." For your boldness and obedience, you are blessed. In the words of my late husband, Elder Joe Brady Brim, Sr., he said repeatedly "That Buster is something else." You see, it's already done!

—Frances Roberts Brim

As a young man I can remember Buster, as we call him, visiting our home in the rural southwest part of Virginia. He was interested in entertaining my sister Hazel. Buster would drive down from New York City in his big, fancy automobile and park it in front of our house. To drive a car of this kind, you had to be a "big shot", or a person of financial means. He would wear sporty clothing and spoke with confidence and as a person of distinction. This was impressive to my family, being southerners. We knew, at that time, that he was a person with great ambitions and dreams of being successful in life.

After a few visits, Buster invited Hazel to New York. Hazel always wanted to leave the farming country and asked our parents for permission to travel to New York to stay with a relative.

Permission was granted, much to her pleasure.

In September 1944, Hazel Roberts and Robuster Strickland were united in holy matrimony, a marriage made in Heaven. I can say that they have been one of the most admired couples in the country. They have been supportive of each other throughout the rearing of their three wonderful children; providing housing for many of their relatives who made their start in the city, including myself, and never forgetting where they came from.

Attending their fiftieth wedding anniversary was a joy and one that we will long remember. Seeing all of the children and grandchildren was a dream come true. God has abundantly blessed

Hazel and Buster have been a blessing to each other, during their sixty years of marriage, as they have been a blessing to others during their lives.

We love them and wish them continued success as they grow in grace and spirit.
> **—Gentry (and Elaine) Roberts, Hazel's brother
> and sister-in-law**

During the early years of Hazel and Robuster's marriage, I was privileged to reside with them in New York until they moved to Arizona. I was very saddened by their move. Nevertheless, we stayed close.

Over the years, I've always known my brother-in-law Buster to be a jovial person who loves to give, help and serve others. Not only does he provide abundantly for his family, but he goes the extra mile to provide for others also. If he knows you need a favor, he will most likely do it before you even ask.

In my summation, I commend Buster for his dedication, perseverance and the difference he has made in so many lives by caring, and sharing with a willing heart and a big smile.

I am truly proud to be his sister-in-law.
> **—Pearl Roberts Abercrombie, Hazel's sister**

My earliest memories of Buster as a little vague because when he was trying to woo my sister Hazel, I was only seven or eight years old.

Years later, all my siblings and I lived in different parts of the country but we always came back to the homeplace for family reunions, anniversaries or just for a visit. Buster loves to tell jokes and at these occasions he kept everyone laughing with his jokes and stories. One thing he specifically likes to do when we are all together is to tell anyone he meets the ages of my sisters and I. He will say, "How old do you think she is?" Or, "Which one do you think is the oldest?" He thinks that bothers us.

No one is ever a stranger to Buster and he will do anything he can for you. He is a kind, giving and unselfish person. I think that is the secret to his blessings and success in life.

I'm glad he's my brother-in-law.

—Mabel Roberts Richardson, Hazel's sister

I am Hazel Roberts Strickland's youngest brother. When I was a ten years old, I noticed this young man, Robuster, coming to our house. I wasn't sure why he kept coming, but it didn't take long to find out; he had a plan to win my sister's heart. After realizing this, I did not like him anymore ...all I could think was, "Robuster is going to take away my sister".

Sure enough, Robuster returned to New York; and, a little later, my sister moved there. It wasn't long before my mother received a letter from my sister. I watched my mother shed a few tears and asked "Mom, why are you crying?" She replied, "Hazel and Robuster are getting married, I am crying for joy."

It is amazing how one can grow up and your love for someone grows up with you. That was in 1944; and since that time, Robuster has given our entire family so much happiness and joy. We all love him greatly; he is woven into the Roberts family as if he was born to be in it. If I had to give him a recommendation, I would say Robuster is the best "brother" anyone could ever have. He's super!

—Aaron Roberts, Hazel's brother

I met Buster at the Heard Museum in downtown Phoenix about forty years ago. Buster was helping to arrange things for a party and I was on the Board at the Museum. I was admiring the Native American art collections at the museum when I spotted his friendly face across the room.

I thought Buster behaved well and I always go by my own instincts; when you see a nice person you just want to say "Hello". I remember telling someone from Barry Goldwater's company that I wanted to meet that young man over there. Buster and I were introduced and have been friends ever since.

After I met Buster, I used to see him in certain places, certain meetings, always around someplace and in the best places. My husband Lloyd Ullman used to invite him to our home to help out at parties a lot, too. Ever since I've known him, Buster was always around, always a part of my life; we're like an extended family.

—Virgina M. Ullman

We have known Buster Strickland for over 40 years. Buster is a wonderful friend and has helped and supported us always. There are no words that can express our gratitude for his many years of service to all of us. He makes taking care of us important and always finds a solution to a problem. Thank God he can get around as well as he does; he always has to remind me that he is older than me. I think our long acquaintance and friendship was best expressed when he and Hazel included us at their 50th wedding celebration. We hope their relationship will continue for a long time.

—John C. Pritzlaff, Jr., former U.S. Ambassador
to Malta and Mary Del Pritzlaff, Philanthropist

I was first introduced to Buster in June 1994 at a party given by his niece Yvonne David. He was quiet, relaxed and had a friendly personality; and even though we had just met him, he and his wife invited my husband and me to their 50th wedding anniversary party, being held in September.

It was a grand affair; his children and grandchildren paid their best respects in song, dance and speeches, as well as dozens of other well-wishers who were obviously very fond of the celebrated couple.

No matter what personal challenges he may be facing, Buster is always happy and warm when he greets you. One day I was in the local supermarket and when I came out he was standing by my car, smiling. He explained that he was waiting to say "hello" and wanted to find out how my husband, who was terminally ill, was feeling.

It's been ten years that I've know Buster; I still run into him at an occasional party and he has not changed; he always greets me with a big smile and makes me feel like I'm part of his extended family.

—Claire Newton, family friend

In the summer of 1998, the man I was dating invited me to dinner at Michael's Restaurant in Mesa where I would meet his Mother and Father. I had no idea that the nervousness I felt would be immediately dissolved by this man who loved and cared about people from every walk of life.

I was introduced to Mr. Buster Strickland. I quickly learned that, with this man, it didn't matter who you were. With or without a title, you were special and had to be a part of his very large family, which includes a lot of people across "the valley" (Phoenix). I learned that many people, who were definitely not related, lovingly referred to Mr. Strickland as "Pa-Pa Buster".

Buster, with his beautiful bride Hazel, would entertain at their home, year after year. During Holidays, Birthdays or Anniversaries, the best place to go was "Buster and Hazel's". Each party would include the invited guests, who would bring their friends, and of course all the Strickland Family would be there; and you might even find the Dr. who performed knee surgery on Buster years ago, attending as well.

As a result of the phone calls from Buster every Sunday, asking, "if I was going to Church?" I found myself attending this huge beautiful Church with their choir singing so loud, you could hear them from the busy street. When you entered the Church, several pews from the front, on the right, you would find Buster and Hazel waiting to tuck you tightly in next to them. Because of their unconditional love and commitment to me, I was baptized in their Church—1st Institutional Baptist Church.

I admire Buster because of a common desire I know many people share. (He is loved by so many). Spending time with Buster, I can tell you, on the day God decides to take this wonderful man home, the town of Phoenix and surrounding towns will shut down to be there and say "goodbye" to a man that shared his life with everyone. What a wonderful legacy he will leave behind!
    —Trisha Ann Garrett, family friend

Buster is my family and he has touched me in many ways with his knowledge and wisdom. I admire him because he is a truly blessed man. I believe that God already has a plan for us and we just need to walk into that plan and purpose. Buster has done that, which is why he is so blessed. He helps people and is concerned about them.

I have been a part of Buster's extended family for many years. I went to school with Kenneth (Buster's son) and I work with the catering business that Buster started many years ago. I like to hear the many stories he tells from the past, particularly the one about how he met and married Hazel.

Buster has been through a lot in his life and I believe he is living the life God would have wanted him to live. I thank him for sharing his wisdom with my family and me.
    —Priscilla Krucko, family friend

I think this book is a great tribute to Mr. Strickland. I met him through a business associate and found him to be a person of great integrity and trustworthiness; and he was always willing to lend a helping hand. I've known him to be a kind, respectable person. My family and I have the utmost respect for Mr. Strickland and his wife Ms. Hazel; and we do believe that behind every good man there is a good woman.

In my twelve plus years of knowing him, Buster has always had some good advice. He uses his experience to help guide those of us who ask, in order to keep us out of the pitfalls.

Mr. Strickland is a wealth of knowledge to draw from; he's not a selfish person. I'd like to share with you this moment of his unselfishness:

Not too long ago, I asked Mr. Strickland to appear and offer a few words at a hearing for my son at 8:30 A.M. He immediately said that he would be there; and asked me when and where. When he arrived, the judge came out and saw Mr. Strickland and smiled. It so happened that Mr. Strickland had helped raise the judge from the time he was a child.

Had it not been for Mr. Strickland's appearance, the outcome for my son would have been far worse than it was; so we are thankful and grateful for him and we think more people should know about him.

We love you Mr. Strickland… keep up the good work.
   —Nazim Muhammad & family, friends

As the owner of Cathy's Rum Cake Caterers, I've been associated with Buster for more than twenty-seven years. I think people should know that there is not a person that comes in Buster's path who needs help or prayers that doesn't get it. Buster knows how to treat people and, in return, he has gained the love and respect of each and every person he comes into contact with.

Buster only sees people—not color, size, race or gender. I've never heard him be unkind to a fellow worker or anyone. He may know all your business, but he minds his own.

I recall an enjoyable moment with Buster when we were at a 50th anniversary party. We had worked together that night and one of the hosts overheard me say to Buster, "I think you are slipping." He asked me what I meant; and I told him that I didn't see Buster's picture on the wall with the rest of the family. Then the hostess said to me "is there a problem?' and I told her "no, but I don't see Buster's picture on the wall. She said, "I'll fix that"; so when they were taking family pictures she said, "Buster, come here." And they took his picture with their family. He and I both laughed as he posed.

Nothing is too big or too little for Buster. He stands tall with the greats and puts his hands out to the oppressed. He never helps people for praise, but just because they need him. He lives life with style, looks good, talks well about others and always knows what to do. The lesson he shows us is to look good, work well and to help others like God wants us to help.

—Cathy Bua, Owner of Cathy's Rum Cakes (Caterers)

Buster! Amazing! He always brought an intense fervor for life wherever I have seen him. Buster knows everyone in the room, and when he speaks to you, you are the only one that matters.

I have always said, "If you want to really know someone, spend time outdoors with them." Go fishing with Buster and find out what he is really like. He puts five lines in the water at a time; he uses five varieties of bait, from cheese to shrimp—taking no chances. Buster sets the hook with all his might, aching and pulling in a harpoon. With a little luck, he catches more than fish—I have seen him catch a fishing reel!

"A lucky man does not chase after luck. A lucky man sets himself up for luck. It will find him, as he chooses to keep moving in optimism, always giving fortune an open target." Buster gave me this advice. I cannot argue with the results that willed his fortune.

—Bennie Bua, family friend

Buster Strickland is family to me and to my family. I don't remember exactly how I met Buster, but suddenly, there he was and I had grown to trust him with my life and all my possessions.

In 1977 I got really lucky and bought a house in Phoenix; it was about 3800 square feet, sitting on 1.6 acres of land. It was built in 1926 and had belonged to the Converse family. In the early 80's I expanded it to 8000 sq feet and included a guesthouse. I had a lot of parties there for charity with sometimes up to 1000 guests, many of who were politicians.

The house was like a museum, filled with many valuables, such as: antiques, precious Kachina dolls, fabulous Indian rugs, prehistoric and historic Indian paintings and cowboy art paintings—valued at over four and a half million dollars. I had to be very careful because when you invite a lot of people to your house, there's always a security issue. Only my wife, son, daughter, bookkeeper, secretary, Buster and I had security codes for the house.

I depended on Buster to help me give my parties. His company would cater the whole event—hors d'oeuvres, dinner, the bar— and his crew even handled the valet parking and the security. Everyone on his team was very professional acting and well-dressed in dark suits and ties; and none of my guests ever had to wait in a line for anything. The society people and politicians of Arizona loved to come to the house and had no problem paying five hundred dollars, one thousand dollars or more for my charity events.

Since then, I've sold the house, but I have great memories and have still kept up my friendship with Buster; and whenever I see Buster or his son Kenny or wife Hazel, I hug them like family. If Buster called upon me at two o'clock in the morning, I'd be there in a heartbeat.

—Chuck Hahn, Businessman, Philanthropist and
Land Developer

The most outstanding attribute of Buster Strickland is his desire to help others. He came to Phoenix as a young man on a stretcher. He was quite ill and overcame so much.

"Uncle Buster" is what my sister Yvonne, my twin brother Bill, and I affectionately call him. He is the most adventurous person I know. Uncle Buster loves a challenge and doesn't hesitate to try out something new. For example, he learned to make wine, became a bee keeper—harvesting the honey, played guitar, was a health food "expert", learned the secret of weight-loss by wearing a special belt, and took college classes later in his life.

There are a thousand stories each of us could share about Buster. Our parents and the Stricklands were like sisters and brothers. We love all of the family.

—Annette Willis, Retired School Teacher
(Roosevelt District)

I first met Robuster "Buster" Strickland in the early 1950's. My wife (Madeline) taught all three of his children in elementary school. Buster and Hazel remained actively involved in their children's progress and activities from elementary school throughout their high school and college years.

Buster and my friendship became even closer due to our affiliation as members of William H. Patterson Lodge #477, which is a subsidiary of the *Improved Benevolent Order of Elks of the World*. Due to his fifty years of service to Elkdom, Buster has been honored with a lifetime membership to this Order.

I have always found "Buster" to be a true reliable friend who can be called upon whether the need is personal, that of the organization, or from the community at large.

One of the highlights of my wife and my 50th wedding anniversary was our dinner/dance affair, which "Buster" and his crew catered for some 75 guests. All the arrangements were superb and made for a celebration which we will remember forever.

Ananias Mason, Retired School Teacher

I met "Bus" when I was hired by the City of Phoenix in 1975. Buster and I were the only employees in the department from New York; and that was one of the similarities we shared. We worked closely on several efficiency studies of various departments.

We spent time together after work, as well as with our families in each other's homes and on picnics with Buster's entire extended family. My two daughters, Dana and Meridith know Buster and worked for Kenny in his catering business; and now even though they have their own families, they still ask about him.

I admire Buster because of his genuine outgoing and warm personality. He makes everyone he meets feel important, from the Governor to his employees. Everyone I know who knows him is taken by his compassion, generosity, and warm personality.

What I think people should know about Buster is his caring of all members of the human race and his ambition to be the best husband, brother, father, grandfather and friend to everyone he meets. I believe he has had a successful life; and I am proud to be his friend.

—Mike Gordon, Arizona State Administrator

In 1986, I was in Arizona on vacation, and met Mr. Robuster Strickland and his lovely wife Hazel at a lawn party at their home. After visiting such a beautiful state, I wanted to return but needed to find a job. When Buster heard that I would come back to live in Arizona if I found work, he had a very prominent family call me in my hometown to make me a job offer that I could not refuse. I moved to Arizona, upon their request, but only to find out that someone else had been hired for my position. Buster felt very bad about this and hired me on the spot to work as a server in the catering business.

Buster and Hazel became my very close friends; they took me to many interesting events, such as the Martin Luther King March in downtown Phoenix, Sedona, the Phoenix First Assembly Christmas Pageant, and…I could go on and on.

Buster has touched my life in many ways, but, the most wonderful way was when he played the role of cupid. I had no dreams that this man would structure my life as he did.

About a year after I moved to Arizona, I was at Buster 's Birthday party. He had many guests there, but made sure that Donald Mallette and I met; fourteen years later, my husband Don and I are still very happy. Don is retired, but with Buster's encouragement, he started a small business/ hobby making Cheese Cakes, which he calls The New York Cheese Cake Factory.

All these wonderful circumstances in my life can be attributed, in some aspect, to my friendship with Buster.

—Bettye Mallette, family friend

...I was seeking part-time work to supplement my full-time income; and as a divorcedsingle parent, I was particular about who and where I wanted to work...I kept getting referred to "Buster Strickland. I was absolutely amazed at his skill level, professional business contacts, the respect that the business contacts have for him, his expectations of his staff, and how much I could learn from just listening and observing Buster.

From a business point of view, I have had a very positive learning experience from Mr. Strickland. On a personal note and out of love, I think of Mr. Buster Strickland and his lovely wife, Mrs. Hazel Strickland as my adopted parents. Getting to know them took me back to the "old school" of when families showed "love for people in their community."

I am grateful that God has blessed me to get to know "Papa" and "Mother Strickland". To know their family is to love them. Many Thanks Papa Buster for creating such a loving and caring family and showing the rest of the world how to put the "L" back in L-O-V-E.

May God's Richest and Best Always Be Yours.
—Fannie Jackson, family friend

I have known Buster Strickland for over fifty years. He is more like an uncle to me because he and his family lived next door to us. He is a very kind-hearted and giving person. When my sisters and I lost both of our parents, Uncle Buster was right there even though it hurt him as much as it hurt us to see them go.

My Dad and I used to go fishing almost every weekend; and Uncle Buster would join us on many occasions. He was noted for his excitement whenever a fish would nibble at his bait. You could hear him in the distance "Gotta bite"! Usually, he pulled in whatever was biting. Uncle Buster also took me on my first dove hunting adventure with his son. When a dove flew over, Uncle Buster fired his shotgun and down came the dove. He sent Kenneth and me out to retrieve the bird, but just as we reached down to pick it up, it jumped up and flew off. Needless to say Kenneth went one way and I went the other way.

There are so many other stories I can share, but I will close by saying what a blessing it is to know Buster Strickland and I thank God for the influence he has had in my life.
—William C. "Bill" Smith III, Family Friend

Buster has been in our family for over 35 years. My husband, Fred Sutter, Sr., worked out in the gym with Buster and then started having him tend bar for his company parties.

After Fred and I got married, Buster was always there whenever we needed him. He was still working, but always had time for our family. If there was a problem all we had to do was call on Buster. We have five boys and they grew up thinking Buster was part of the family.

When my husband was so sick, Buster was a great help with taking my husband to the doctor if I was busy or needed a break. He would come over 4-5 times a week just to sit and talk with Fred; or if he felt up to it, Buster would take him out for a ride and to do errands.

He has always been nothing but kind to this family and we love him to no end.

—Judy Sutter and Family, Dan Schwartz Realty, Inc.

I have been a friend of the Stricklands for many years. What a great family! There's only one Buster; he's very unique. Everyone loves him; he has a very outgoing personality and is a real people person...with lots of energy.

Buster is always the first one to help someone in trouble; no one has a bigger heart.

—Margie McHarg—a great friend

About the Author

The son of a sharecropper, Robuster Strickland surpassed many obstacles during his youth, growing up as one of his father's twenty children. Born in Patrick County, Virginia "Buster" moved to Long Island, New York when he was two years old. His family continued to work on farms raising fruits and vegetables and tending to cows, pigs and other animals. Buster depended on farming as a way of life until he completed high school.

Since his childhood, Buster was plagued with chronic asthma, which challenged him throughout his youth. At the age of eighteen, Buster was drafted into the army, but because of his asthma, was honorably discharged before he completed basic training. Though he loved being around nature—farming, hunting and fishing—he eventually changed his career path to transportation work, which seemed to keep his asthma more under control.

When he was twenty-five years old, happily married to Hazel and raising a three-year-old daughter, Buster's life changed suddenly. After being hospitalized for several weeks, following a near-fatal bout of asthma and being told that unless he moved immediately, he would only have a year to live, Buster bravely uprooted his young family; and in an effort to prolong his life, moved to Phoenix, Arizona in 1949.

While living in Phoenix, Buster has experienced many firsts: He was the first black truck driver for the Maricopa County Highway Department in Phoenix; he was the first black chief inspector for the City of Phoenix Streets and Sanitation Department; and he retired from his position as the City of Phoenix's first black management analyst.

Along with wages from his regular employment, Buster also fed his growing family by using his childhood skills. He grew vegetables and fruits, raised goats and chickens, kept bees; and went fishing in the nearby lakes, whenever time permitted. Since he was a youngster, helping his mother in the kitchen, Buster has loved to cook and continues to share his delectable dishes with many friends and family members. Although Buster now has a smaller garden, since the children have grown up, he still loves to grow his own vegetables.

Buster is known as an active gem in the city of Phoenix because he wants to help everyone he meets. He has been a member of the First Institutional Baptist Church since 1949, where he sang in the choir and served on the Board of Trustees. He also serves on the Board of Trustees at Wesley Community Center-Phoenix and the Elks Lodge, as well as on the Board of Directors at Ebony House.

In addition to his community involvement, Buster is a strong leader and mentor who initiates a variety of family activities with his wife Hazel Strickland, three children—Marilyn, Rochelle and Kenneth and his grandchildren.

Among his many honors and awards, Robuster "Buster" Strickland received the 2004 *Ageless Hero Award for Vigor and Vitality* presented by Blue Cross and Blue Shield of Arizona and the Arizona Republic.

About the Co-author

Yvonne Rose is the Vice President and Senior Editor of Amber Communications Group, Inc. The Company's imprints include: Amber Books, Busta Books, Colossus Books, Ambrosia Books, Amber/Wiley Books and Amber Books2.

Yvonne entered the world of book publishing when she (a former model) and her husband Tony Rose co-wrote the national bestseller *Is Modeling for You – The Handbook & Guide for the Young Aspiring Black Model*. Mr. Rose published Amber Books' flagship title *in 1998*.

Amber Communications Group, Inc. has become the nation's largest African American publisher of self-help books and celebrity bios and is the recipient of several awards, including: the *Chicago Black Book Fair and Conference Independent Publisher/Press Award* of the Year, as well as the *2003 BlackBoard BestSeller's African-American Publisher of the Year Award* and the *2003 American Library Association "Reluctant Reader Award"*.

Yvonne has served as editor for several titles in the ACGI catalogue, including: *Fighting for Your Life: The African-American Criminal Justice Survival Guide; The African-American Teenager's Guide to Personal Growth, Health, Safety, Sex and Survival; 101 Real Money Questions—The African-American Financial Question and Answer Book; Beautiful Black Hair; The Afrocentric Bride—A Styling Guide; Born Beautiful —The African-American Teenager's Complete Beauty Guide and Wake Up and Smell the Dollars! Whose Inner City is This Anyway*!

Prior to entering the book publishing industry, Yvonne worked as a freelance publicist, contributing writer and editor for several national magazines, including: *Black Elegance, Sophisticate's Black Hair Care, Hype Hair, Unique Hair and Beauty, Right On!* and *CLASS*. She is also an award-winning journalist with features appearing in *Kip Business Report, Network Journal and Harlem News*.

For further information, visit: WWW.AMBERBOOKS.COM or email: amberbks@aol.com.

Order Form

Strickland Books

Send checks or money orders to:
Robuster Strickland
13005 S. 37th St.
Phoenix, AZ 85044

Please send _____ copy(ies) of *Led By the Spirit* to:

Name: _____

Address:_____

City:_____

State:_____Zip:_____

Telephone: (____)_____

Email: _____

I have enclosed $16.95 per book, plus $4.00 shipping per book for a total of $_____.

Sales tax: Add 7.05% to total book cost for orders shipped to Arizona addresses.

For Bulk or Wholesale Rates, call: 480-460-6904